Rose Elliot's
PASTA

Rose Elliot's

VEGETARIAN PASTA

·

150 MOUTHWATERING DISHES
FROM THE EXPERT

HarperCollins*Illustrated*

With book sales of three million, Rose Elliot is Britain's bestselling vegetarian cookery author. She has earned the praise of vegetarians and non-vegetarians alike for the originality and imaginativeness of her recipes.

Her first book, *Simply Delicious*, published in 1967, was written in response to the many requests she received from visitors to the retreat centre run by her parents, where she then cooked. The book was widely praised and, since then, Rose has written many bestsellers.

Rose frequently contributes to national magazines, gives cookery demonstrations and broadcasts on radio and television. She lives with her husband, Robert, and youngest daughter, Claire, in Hampshire. Rose has always had a great interest in astrology and has practised this alongside her career as a cookery writer. With Robert she runs a computer-based astrological service which provides high quality personality profiles, forecasts and compatibility charts. More details can be obtained from: Rose Elliot Horoscopes, PO Box 16, Eastleigh, Hampshire SO50 5YP.

First published in 1997 by HarperCollins*Publishers*

This paperback edition published in 1999 by HarperCollins*Illustrated*
Reprinted 2000 , 2001
The HarperCollins website address is www.**fire**and**water**.com

Text © Rose Elliot 1997
Photographs © HarperCollins*Publishers* 1997
All rights reserved

Editor: Mari Roberts
Photographer: Patrice de Villiers
Home Economist: Meg Yansz
Stylist: Penny Markham
Indexer: Susan Bosanko

A catalogue record for this book is available from the British Library

ISBN 0 00 414076 1

Typeset in Gill Sans and Goudy
Colour reproduction by Colourscan, Singapore
Printed and bound in Italy

CONTENTS

Introduction

During the last few years the growing popularity of vegetarianism and of pasta have gone hand in hand. Things have certainly changed since I was a child when vegetarians were few and far between and pasta meant spaghetti out of a tin or macaroni cheese. And pasta is certainly an excellent food for vegetarians: it provides a starting point for a meal that does not involve having to soak beans or grind nuts, and it is something that we can confidently share with our friends, knowing that they will enjoy the results.

From the nutritional point of view, pasta has much to recommend it. It is what is known as a 'complex carbohydrate', one of the group of foods which nutritionists rate highly and urge us to make into the basis of our meals, along with plenty of fresh fruit and vegetables and modest amounts of protein. If the dish does not contain vegetables, I usually serve it with a leafy salad, or start or finish the meal with fresh fruit, because I do believe that one of the secrets of healthy eating is to eat at least the amount of fresh fruit and vegetables recommended by the World Health Organization (400g/14oz per day), and preferably more.

For the most part, the recipes in this book do not claim to be authentically Italian, although some of them are. They are mostly dishes that have evolved when I have been cooking for my friends and family, or that other people have made for me, and which have worked well and been enjoyed. I hope that you will like them, and that you will remember that there is always room for your own experimentation too, particularly with something easy-going like pasta.

With my very best wishes, and happy eating,

Rose Elliot

ROSE ELLIOT

Pasta Basics

Cheap to buy, convenient to store, easy to cook, versatile to use, great to eat, good for you and always increasing in popularity, pasta might truly be described as the food of the twenty-first century.

The range of pasta available is becoming more extensive all the time. In Italy there are literally hundreds of different shapes, often with inspired and imaginative names, such as 'elephant's teeth' and 'angel's hair', and even 'priest stranglers'. The name by which a pasta shape is known often varies from region to region: this is confusing, but it is also one of the charms of cooking with Italian pasta.

Each shape of pasta has a subtly different role to play and real pasta aficionados take great care in matching the pasta to the right sauce. An Italian might say that this is an innate skill which is difficult for a non-Italian to learn. However, as you experiment with different shapes and sauces, you will develop an instinct for matching pasta and sauce, at least to your own taste. I firmly believe that part of the joy of cooking lies in feeling relaxed and confident enough to try different flavours and combinations for yourself without feeling worried about what is 'right' and 'wrong'. Here are some basic guidelines to help you when making your choice of pasta.

CHOOSING PASTA

Long pastas, such as spaghetti, work best with smooth sauces that will cling to them; a sauce with chunky pieces is difficult to eat with long, slippery strands. The exception to this rule is the long fusilli pasta (fusilli lunghi), a long coiled pasta which catches chunky pieces in its curls.

Ribbon pastas, which include tagliatelle, pappardelle and fettuccine, are delicate and porous. They are all very good with creamy sauces, although pappardelle, being so wide, is complemented by strong flavours.

Short tubes such as penne and rigatoni are adaptable. These are perhaps the best 'all round' pastas and go well with a number of different sauces, including cream ones. They trap the sauce in their cavities, making it easy to eat, and they are also good with chunky ingredients.

Special shapes such as conchiglie (shells), fusilli (spirals), farfalle (butterflies or bow ties), lumache (snails) and so on are also perfect for mixing with chunky ingredients and great in pasta salads. Remember that the pasta called gnocchi is named after the small potato dumpling whose shape it copies; if you ask for gnocchi you may get potato dumplings instead. (You need to ask for the pasta version.)

Soup pastas are tiny and include many pretty shapes such as stelline (little stars), farfalline (baby butterflies), alfabetini (little letters of the alphabet), and orzi, which look like grains of rice.

As well as the Italian pastas, there are also oriental noodles. I have included a couple of recipes using these, concentrating on the ones that are widely available. They are prepared differently from Italian pasta, requiring only a soaking in boiling water before use. Like pasta, they are good for quickly turning a stir-fry or soup into a more substantial dish.

Pasta is now available in flavours such as beetroot, saffron, truffle, tomato and basil, as well as the familiar spinach which creates pasta verde or green pasta. These pastas look beautiful, especially before they are cooked, but, with the exception of spinach pasta, their flavour does not contribute anything to the dish, and they are not used in Italy.

Pasta is made from wheat, but if you cannot eat wheat, or prefer not to, try corn and rice pastas. These are available in coloured and flavoured versions, which seem to be more successful than those of their wheat counterpart. Corn and rice pastas are available from health shops or by mail order. Some of them taste surprisingly good. Careful cooking is required: they go from hard to soggy in a matter of moments and I find that they take far less time to cook than is suggested on the packaging.

FRESH OR DRIED PASTA?

Fresh pasta is widely available, but unless it is made on the spot by a skilled pasta-maker and purchased freshly made, it often turns out heavy and disappointing. Pasta does not take kindly to being refrigerated; drying is a far better way of preserving it, which is why, generally, dried pasta is a far better buy than so-called 'fresh', and the more you pay for the dried pasta, usually, the better it is.

Stuffed pasta, such as ravioli, tortellini and cappelletti, have to be bought fresh but here again you need to be selective – some of them can be very heavy. I have not included recipes for using these pastas because they are best served simply with butter or olive oil and crushed garlic or chopped herbs, or else with a light sauce such as fresh tomato.

COOKING PASTA

Allow roughly 100g / 3½oz of pasta for each person. For every 100g allow 1 litre of water and ¾ teaspoon of salt when cooking. So, you will need:

For 2 people
200g / 7oz pasta, 2 litres / 3½ pints of water, 1½ teaspoons of salt

For 4 people
400g / 14oz pasta, 4 litres / 7 pints of water, 3 teaspoons (1 tablespoon) of salt

Use a large saucepan so that the pasta can move around as it cooks. First bring the saucepan of water to the boil, then add the pasta along with the salt. Cover the pan briefly, then, when the water comes back to the boil (this happens quickly), remove the lid and let the pasta continue at a rolling boil until it is 'al dente' – just tender but with a firm bite. This may take less time than that stated on the packet, so start testing, by lifting out a piece of pasta and biting it, in good time. It will be hot, so blow on it first! In the recipes in this book I have mostly given an average time of 8 minutes but you should always use your own judgement and always test the pasta after the first few minutes have gone by.

When the pasta is done, tip it into a colander and shake it gently to remove excess water. You do not need to get the pasta dry, indeed it is better to leave some water still clinging to it. Then you can either put the pasta into a large warmed bowl with some olive oil and any other ingredients you are using, or you can do as I do and tip it back into the still-warm saucepan before adding the oil and other additions and tossing well.

Either way, quickly put the pasta onto warmed plates – pasta cools down rapidly – add toppings if you are using any and serve immediately, *presto, pronto* and *buon appetito!*

Fusilli lunghi

Lasagnette

Pappardelle

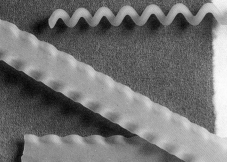

Ruote di carro

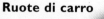

There are hundreds of different pasta shapes and some of them have several names which vary in Italy from area to area. So putting a name to a shape can be a little confusing; however, you can often substitute another similar pasta shape in a recipe if necessary. In this book I have used pasta which is quite widely available so finding a particular variety should not pose too many problems. Here and on the next two pages are shown the pasta shapes which are used in the recipes; if you cannot find exactly the type specified, at least you will know roughly what you are looking for and will be able to buy something similar! I have always found specialist Italian shops very helpful in tracking down particular types of pasta or suggesting alternatives and it is always fun to try something new.

Pastine

Farfalline

Egg noodles

Quick guide to Pasta

•

Stelline

Lumache

Spaghetti

Fusilli

Vermicelli

Macaroni

Lasagne

Fettuccine

Pipe rigate

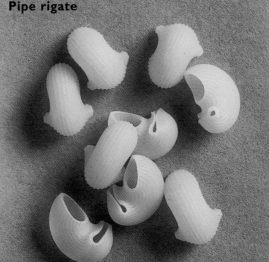

Penne rigate

Orecchiette

Farfalle

Tagliatelle

Pennoni

Gnocchi

Penne

Rigatoni

Conchiglie rigate

Spaghettini

Pasta Soups

Almost any soup can be made more filling and nutritious by the addition of a handful of pasta. You do not need a great deal: 50–100g / 2–4oz for a soup to serve four people is ample. It is a great way of turning a simple soup into a main course.

Tiny soup pastas come in many different shapes and it is fun to try different ones. Children particularly enjoy finding interesting pasta shapes in their food and a vegetable soup with pasta in it and perhaps a little grated cheese over the top can be a great way to tempt faddy eaters or vegetable-haters.

There are a number of thick and filling soups in this section: Provençal pistou, Tuscan white bean and pasta soup with garlic croûtons, and Middle-eastern spiced lentil and pasta soup, for instance. Serve with bread and perhaps a side salad as a satisfying main course.

A pasta soup can also be light and delicate, and make an excellent first course. Leek, parsley and pasta broth, Thai coconut soup with noodles, and Fresh tomato soup with farfalline and basil come into this category; they are refreshing and ideal to whet your appetite.

Some of these soups call for stock and, of course, homemade is best if you have it. Otherwise buy a good stock from the supermarket, or a good quality vegetable (vegetarian) stock cube or (my favourite) a Swiss vegetable bouillon powder.

HARVEST VEGETABLE AND PASTA SOUP Serves ❹

INGREDIENTS

3 tablespoons olive oil

1 onion, peeled and chopped

1 garlic clove, peeled and crushed

450g / 1lb peeled and de-seeded pumpkin, diced

225g / 8oz carrots, scraped and cut into 6mm / ¼ inch slices

175g / 6oz sweetcorn kernels, cut from the cob or frozen

1.2 litres / 2 pints vegetable stock

225g / 8oz courgettes, trimmed and cut into 6mm / ¼ inch slices

50g / 2oz small pasta shapes

salt and freshly ground black pepper

4 tablespoons roughly chopped fresh parsley, preferably flat-leaf, to serve

This soup makes the most of the late summer harvest of sweetcorn, pumpkin and carrot, to produce a gloriously golden soup made more substantial with the addition of pasta. Some hot crunchy garlic or herb bread goes well with it, or you could serve it with chunks of wholewheat bread and some grated cheese – either a strong vegetarian Cheddar or freshly grated Parmesan cheese.

1 Heat the oil in a large saucepan, put in the onion, garlic, pumpkin and carrots, stir briefly, then cover and leave to cook gently for 10–15 minutes, until the vegetables start to become soft.

2 Add the sweetcorn kernels and the stock to the pan. Bring to the boil, then lower the heat and leave to simmer over a gentle heat for about 20 minutes.

3 Add the courgettes to the soup, bring back to the boil and simmer for 5 minutes. Then add the pasta and cook for a further 8 minutes.

4 Season with salt and pepper, then serve into warm bowls and top each with plenty of parsley.

TUSCAN WHITE BEAN AND PASTA SOUP WITH GARLIC CROÛTONS Serves ❹

INGREDIENTS

olive oil

1 onion, peeled and chopped

2 garlic cloves, peeled and crushed

2 x 400g / 14oz cans cannellini beans

1.2 litres / 2 pints vegetable stock

4 thick slices of bread, crusts removed

50g / 2oz small pasta shapes

salt and freshly ground black pepper

So simple and easy, yet filling and good to eat. The crunchy garlic croûtons make a nice touch, but if you have not time to do them, just serve the soup with chunks of bread.

1 Heat 2 tablespoons of olive oil in a large saucepan, put in the onion and half the garlic, stir briefly, then cover and leave to cook gently for 10 minutes, until the onion is becoming soft.

2 Add the beans, together with their liquid, and the stock. Bring to the boil, then lower the heat and leave to simmer for 20 minutes.

3 Meanwhile, make the croûtons. Rub the surface of the bread with the remaining garlic, then fry the bread on both sides in a little hot olive oil, until crisp and golden. Cut into small squares and keep on one side.

4 Add the pasta shapes to the soup, bring back to the boil and simmer for 6–8 minutes until the pasta is cooked. Season with salt and pepper, then serve into warm bowls and top each with some croûtons.

MIDDLE-EASTERN SPICED LENTIL AND PASTA SOUP Serves ❹

INGREDIENTS

3 tablespoons olive oil

2 onions, peeled and chopped

2 garlic cloves, peeled and crushed

125g / 4oz split red lentils

1.2 litres / 2 pints vegetable stock

50g / 2oz small pasta shapes

1 tablespoon ground coriander

1 tablespoon ground cumin

squeeze of lemon juice

salt and freshly ground black pepper

4 tablespoons roughly chopped fresh coriander, to serve

Tasty and comforting, this soup is good served with warmed poppadums or other Indian breads.

1 Heat the oil in a large saucepan, put in the onion and garlic, stir briefly, then cover and leave to cook gently for 10 minutes, until the onion is becoming soft. Transfer about a third of the mixture to a smaller saucepan and leave on one side for the moment.

2 Add the lentils and the stock to the onions in the large saucepan. Bring to the boil, then lower the heat and leave to simmer for 30 minutes. Add the pasta and cook for a further 8 minutes.

3 Meanwhile, reheat the onion and garlic in the smaller saucepan, then stir in the coriander and cumin. Cook for 1 minute, stirring, then remove from the heat and add to the soup, along with a squeeze of lemon juice and salt and pepper to taste.

4 Serve the soup into warm bowls and top each with a good spoonful of chopped fresh coriander.

THAI COCONUT SOUP WITH NOODLES Serves ❹

INGREDIENTS

1 stalk of lemon grass, finely chopped

2.5cm / 1 inch piece of fresh ginger, grated

1 fresh green chilli, de-seeded and finely chopped

1 kaffir lime leaf if available, or a piece of lime rind

a 425g / 15oz can coconut milk

60g Chinese egg noodles

225g / 8oz baby sweetcorn, cut into 1cm / ½ inch pieces

juice of 1 lime

salt and freshly ground black pepper

4–6 tablespoons chopped fresh coriander, to serve

This attractive soup is delicate and creamy, with hot and sour Thai flavourings. I use the kind of noodles that come pressed into a block, but you could also use other thin, quick-cooking varieties.

1 Put the lemon grass, ginger, chilli and lime leaf or lime rind into a saucepan with 600ml / 1 pint of water. Bring to the boil, then cover the pan and simmer gently for 15 minutes, for the water to absorb all the flavours.

2 Next, either scoop out and discard the lemon grass, ginger, chilli and lime leaf or rind, squeezing as much water from them as possible first, or keep them in the soup, depending on your taste – I like to keep them in.

3 Add the coconut milk to the pan and bring to the boil, then put in the noodles and sweetcorn and cook for a further 2–3 minutes, until the noodles are soft.

4 Add lime juice, and salt and pepper to taste. Serve into warm bowls with a generous sprinkling of chopped fresh coriander on each.

WOODLAND MUSHROOM AND PASTA SOUP Serves ❹

INGREDIENTS

6g dried porcini mushrooms

2 tablespoons olive oil

I onion, peeled and chopped

I garlic clove, peeled and crushed

450g / Ilb assorted fresh mushrooms, including wild ones if available, washed and roughly chopped

I litre / 1¾ pints vegetable stock

50g / 2oz small pasta shapes

salt and freshly ground black pepper

2 tablespoons chopped fresh parsley, preferably flat-leaf, to serve

Assorted wild mushrooms, sometimes sold by the bag in supermarkets, are great for this soup. It is also a wonderful way to celebrate a successful mushroom foray in the woods. Otherwise, make up your own selection of mushrooms from whatever is available, or use all one type – field mushrooms if you can get them, but even ordinary cultivated mushrooms are good.

1 Put the dried porcini mushrooms into a small bowl and cover with 150ml / 5fl oz boiling water. Leave for 15–30 minutes to soak. Then drain them, catching and reserving the liquid. Chop the mushrooms.

2 Heat the oil in a large saucepan, put in the onion and garlic, stir briefly, then cover and leave to cook gently for 10 minutes, until the onions start to become soft.

3 Add the fresh mushrooms and the soaked mushrooms to the onions. Stir, then cook, uncovered, for 15 minutes or so until the mushrooms are completely tender.

4 Pour in the stock, then add the reserved mushroom liquid, pouring it through a fine strainer or a piece of muslin to catch any grit (with the packaged porcini now available it is unusual to find any, but best be on the safe side). Bring to the boil, then lower the heat and leave to simmer for 5 minutes.

5 Put in the pasta and cook for a further 6–8 minutes until done. Then season the soup and serve it into warm bowls with parsley scattered on top of each.

FRESH TOMATO SOUP WITH FARFALLINE AND BASIL Serves ❹

INGREDIENTS

2 tablespoons olive oil

I onion, peeled and chopped

I garlic clove, peeled and crushed

Ikg / 2lb fresh tomatoes, skinned and roughly chopped

600ml / I pint vegetable stock

50g / 2oz farfalline or other small pasta shapes

salt and freshly ground black pepper

fresh basil leaves, to serve

This is a light and refreshing pasta soup which makes the most of the flavour of summer tomatoes, especially if you have plenty in the garden. It is nice for summer lunch, followed by a garden salad.

1 Heat the oil in a large saucepan, put in the onion and garlic, stir briefly, then cover and leave to cook gently for 10 minutes, until the onions start to become soft.

2 Add the tomatoes, stir, then cover and cook for a further 10–15 minutes, until the tomatoes have collapsed.

3 Add the stock, bring to the boil, then lower the heat and leave to simmer for 5 minutes. Then put in the farfalline and cook for a further 5–8 minutes.

4 Season the soup to taste, then serve it into warm bowls. Tear some fresh basil leaves over each one.

LEEK, PARSLEY AND PASTA BROTH Serves ❹

INGREDIENTS

2 tablespoons olive oil

700g / 1½lb leeks, trimmed and cut into 6mm / ¼ inch slices

1 garlic clove, peeled and crushed

1.2 litres / 2 pints vegetable stock

75g / 3oz small pasta shapes

4 – 6 tablespoons chopped fresh parsley, preferably flat-leaf

salt and freshly ground black pepper

freshly grated Parmesan cheese, to serve

The better the vegetable stock you use for this broth, the better this soup will be. Homemade stock is best if you have time to make it; otherwise, buy a good vegetable stock or bouillon powder or concentrate – it is worth trying different brands in small quantities to find your favourite.

1 Heat the oil in a large saucepan and put in the leeks and garlic. Stir briefly, then cover and leave the vegetables to cook gently for 10–15 minutes, until the leeks start to become soft. Stir the contents of the pan from time to time to prevent sticking.

2 Add the stock, stir, then cook for a further 10–15 minutes. Add the pasta, bring to the boil and cook for 8–10 minutes more.

3 Stir in the parsley, season with salt and pepper, then serve into warm bowls and hand round the Parmesan.

SUMMER GARDEN PASTA SOUP WITH FRESH HERBS Serves ❹

INGREDIENTS

2 tablespoons olive oil

1 onion, peeled and chopped

1 garlic clove, peeled and crushed

225g / 8oz young carrots, thinly sliced

1.2 litres / 2 pints vegetable stock

125g / 4oz podded fresh peas

125g / 4oz podded fresh broad beans

125g / 4oz young green beans, cut into 2.5cm / 1 inch lengths

125g / 4oz courgettes, trimmed and thinly sliced

50g / 2oz small pasta shapes

salt and freshly ground black pepper

4 tablespoons chopped fresh herbs: parsley, chives and mint

freshly grated Parmesan cheese, to serve

Easy and quick to do, this makes an effortless light meal for an early summer day. You can vary the vegetables according to what is available. Serve it with warmed bread or rolls or hot garlic or herb bread, and maybe a glass of chilled white wine. Complete the seasonal meal with some summer fruits, simply prepared: black cherries, strawberries or raspberries with some thick Greek yoghurt or crème fraîche, if you like, or a gooseberry fool or summer pudding.

1 Heat the oil in a large saucepan, put in the onion, garlic and carrots, stir briefly, then cover and leave to cook gently for 10 minutes, until the vegetables start to become soft but don't overcook them.

2 Add the stock and bring to the boil, then add the peas, broad beans, green beans and courgettes. Bring back to the boil, then add the pasta shapes and cook for about 6–8 minutes, until the vegetables and pasta are cooked.

3 Season with salt and pepper, stir in the herbs, then serve into warm bowls and top each with a good spoonful of Parmesan.

PROVENÇAL PISTOU Serves ❹

INGREDIENTS

3 tablespoons olive oil

1 onion, peeled and chopped

1 garlic clove, peeled and crushed

1 leek, trimmed and cut into 6mm / ¼ inch slices

2 celery sticks, trimmed and chopped

225g / 8oz carrots, scraped and cut into 6mm / ¼ inch slices

a 400g / 14oz can chickpeas

1.2 litres / 2 pints vegetable stock

4 fresh tomatoes, skinned and chopped

1 medium courgette, trimmed and cut into 6mm / ¼ inch slices

50g / 2oz small pasta shapes, e.g. farfallini

4 tablespoons pesto sauce: a good bought one, or see page 76

salt and freshly ground black pepper

freshly grated Parmesan cheese, to serve

There are many versions of this tasty soup from southern France. They are all based on a vegetable soup that includes chickpeas, with pasta and pesto added towards the end of the cooking time. It is a wonderfully hearty, 'meal in itself' kind of soup; the only accompaniment it needs is some good bread and perhaps a glass of wine.

1 Heat the oil in a large saucepan, put in the onion, garlic, leek, celery and carrots, stir briefly, then cover and leave to cook gently for 10–15 minutes, until the vegetables start to become soft.

2 Add the chickpeas, together with their liquid, and the stock. Bring to the boil, then lower the heat and leave to simmer for 20 minutes.

3 Add the tomatoes and courgette to the soup, bring back to the boil and simmer for 5 minutes. Then add the pasta and cook for a further 10 minutes.

4 Stir in the pesto sauce, check the seasoning, then serve into warm bowls and top each with a good spoonful of Parmesan.

Pasta Salads

I found this one of the most enjoyable sections of the book to write. I love salads anyway, but I particularly liked having the chance to experiment with different combinations including pasta. As with soups, when you add pasta to a salad it becomes more filling and turns immediately from a side dish into something more serious. I soon realized that you can add pasta to almost any salad, with good results. Pasta salads are best eaten warm or at room temperature. They can be allowed to get cool, but they are best not refrigerated as the cold air tends to make them heavy.

Pasta salads are good additions to a group of salads for a party; they are useful for serving with a light main course to make a more substantial meal; they make brilliant first courses, and, as I have said, can be main courses in their own right. If you are serving a pasta salad as a main course, offer warm bread with it, and perhaps another, more simple salad, made from an ingredient that is not included in the pasta salad: tomato, green leaves or grated carrot tossed in vinaigrette with chopped herbs or spring onion, for example.

When making salads, use the best flavouring ingredients you can. The better the olive oil and vinegar that you use, the better the salad will be, and you only need small amounts. I like to use good quality extra virgin olive oil and red wine vinegar for salads.

FARFALLE SALAD WITH ASPARAGUS AND NEW PEAS IN MINT VINAIGRETTE Serves ❹

INGREDIENTS

400g / 14oz farfalle

salt

450g / 1lb asparagus, trimmed and halved to make pieces about 5cm / 2 inches long

225g / 8oz shelled fresh peas

3 tablespoons olive oil

1 tablespoon wine vinegar

freshly ground black pepper

2 tablespoons freshly chopped or torn mint

A delicious, refreshing salad for summer, perfect with a glass of chilled white wine.

1 Fill a large saucepan with 4 litres / 7 pints of water and put it on the stove to heat up for the pasta.

2 When the water boils, add the pasta along with a tablespoon of salt and give the pasta a quick stir. Briefly put the lid on until it starts to lift, showing that the water has come back to the boil, then let the pasta bubble away, uncovered, for about 8 minutes, or until it is tender but still has some bite to it.

3 Meanwhile, cook the asparagus in a little boiling water until just tender: 6–8 minutes. A minute before it is done, put in the peas. Drain the asparagus and peas.

4 Make a vinaigrette by putting the oil, vinegar and a seasoning of salt and pepper into a jar and shaking until combined.

5 Drain the pasta by tipping it all into a colander placed in the sink, then put it back into the still-warm pan. Add the asparagus, peas and mint. Give the vinaigrette a quick shake, then add to the pasta and stir gently until everything is coated. Serve immediately, or cover and leave until the salad cools to room temperature.

PENNE RIGATE SALAD WITH SUN-DRIED TOMATOES, ARTICHOKE HEARTS, BASIL AND PARMESAN Serves ❹

INGREDIENTS

400g / 14oz penne rigate

salt

3 tablespoons olive oil

1 tablespoon wine vinegar

½ teaspoon Dijon mustard

1 garlic clove, peeled and crushed

freshly ground black pepper

a 400g / 14oz can artichoke hearts, drained and sliced

8 sun-dried tomatoes, chopped

125g / 4oz fresh Parmesan cheese, cut in flakes

4 good sprigs of fresh basil, torn

I find canned artichoke hearts useful in pasta dishes – I love their piquant flavour – but you could also use artichokes that have been bottled in oil. In this case, use some of the oil to make the vinaigrette, and go easy on the vinegar, because the flavour may not need much sharpening.

1 Fill a large saucepan with 4 litres / 7 pints of water and put it on the stove to heat up for the pasta.

2 When the water boils, add the pasta along with a tablespoon of salt and give the pasta a quick stir. Briefly put the lid on until it starts to lift, showing that the water has come back to the boil, then let the pasta bubble away, uncovered, for about 8 minutes, or until it is tender but still has some bite to it.

3 Make a vinaigrette by putting the oil, vinegar, mustard, garlic and a seasoning of salt and pepper into a jar and shaking until thoroughly combined.

4 Drain the pasta by tipping it all into a colander placed in the sink, then put it back into the still-warm pan. Add the artichoke hearts, sun-dried tomatoes, Parmesan and basil. Give the vinaigrette a quick shake, then add to the pasta and stir gently until everything is coated. Serve immediately, or cover and leave until the salad cools to room temperature.

PENNE WITH GRILLED MIXED PEPPERS IN SUN-DRIED TOMATO VINAIGRETTE Serves ❹

This is a salad of vibrant colours and flavours. Serve it with warm ciabatta bread.

1 Fill a large saucepan with 4 litres / 7 pints of water and put it on the stove to heat up for the pasta.

2 Next prepare the peppers by cutting them into quarters and placing, skin-side (shiny-side) up, on a grill pan. Put under a high heat for 10–15 minutes, until the skin has blistered and blackened in places. Cover the peppers with a plate and leave until cool enough to handle, then remove the skin, stem and seeds, and cut the flesh into strips.

3 When the water in the saucepan boils, add the pasta along with a tablespoon of salt and give the pasta a quick stir. Briefly put the lid on until it starts to lift, showing that the water has come back to the boil, then let the pasta bubble away, uncovered, for about 8 minutes, or until it is tender but still has some bite to it.

4 Make a vinaigrette by putting the oil, sun-dried tomato purée, vinegar, garlic and a seasoning of salt and pepper into a jar and shaking until combined.

5 Drain the pasta by tipping it all into a colander placed in the sink, then put it back into the still-warm pan. Add the peppers. Give the vinaigrette a quick shake, then add to the pasta and stir gently until coated. Serve immediately, or cover and leave until the salad cools to room temperature. Scatter with basil and Parmesan before serving.

COLD NOODLE SALAD Serves ❹

The roasted sesame oil used in this recipe really makes the flavour, and the soft noodles contrast well with the crisp vegetables. If you cannot get rice vinegar, which is delicate and light, use a squeeze of lemon juice instead.

1 Bring a kettleful of water to the boil. Put the noodles into a large bowl or saucepan, cover generously with boiling water and leave for 2–3 minutes (or according to the instructions on the packet) until tender, then drain them.

2 Pour the noodles into a serving bowl and add the roasted sesame oil, soy sauce, rice vinegar and garlic. Toss together gently to mix well.

3 Cook the mangetout and sweetcorn together in a little boiling water for 1–2 minutes until just tender. Drain, refresh under the cold tap and drain again.

4 Add the mangetout and sweetcorn to the noodles, along with the spring onions, coriander and salt and pepper to taste. Serve immediately, or cover and leave until the salad cools to room temperature. In either case, add the peanuts, if using, just before you serve the salad.

FARFALLE SALAD WITH GRUYÈRE, CHERRY TOMATOES AND SPRING ONIONS Serves ❹

INGREDIENTS

bunch of spring onions, trimmed and cut into long ribbons

400g / 14oz farfalle

salt

3 tablespoons olive oil

1 tablespoon wine vinegar

½ teaspoon Dijon mustard

freshly ground black pepper

225g / 8oz cherry tomatoes, halved

125g / 4oz Gruyère cheese, diced or coarsely grated

2 tablespoons freshly chopped or torn flat-leaf parsley

Serve this salad with soft granary rolls or ciabatta bread and a green salad on the side for a complete light meal.

1 Fill a large saucepan with 4 litres / 7 pints of water and put it on the stove to heat up for the pasta.

2 Meanwhile, put the spring onion ribbons into icy-cold water and leave on one side to curl.

3 When the water in the saucepan boils, add the pasta along with a tablespoon of salt and give the pasta a quick stir. Briefly put the lid on until it starts to lift, showing that the water has come back to the boil, then let the pasta bubble away, uncovered, for about 8 minutes, or until it is tender but still has some bite to it.

4 Make a vinaigrette by putting the oil, vinegar, mustard and a seasoning of salt and pepper into a jar and shaking until thoroughly combined.

5 Drain the pasta by tipping it all into a colander placed in the sink, then put it back into the still-warm pan. Drain the spring onions and add them to the pasta along with the tomatoes, Gruyère and parsley. Give the vinaigrette a quick shake, then add to the pasta and stir gently until everything is coated. Serve immediately, or cover and leave until the salad cools to room temperature.

PENNE RIGATE SALAD WITH MAYONNAISE, CELERY, APPLE AND TOASTED PINE NUTS Serves ❹

INGREDIENTS

50g / 2oz raisins

400g / 14oz penne rigate

salt

2 sweet apples

1 tablespoon lemon juice

3 tablespoons mayonnaise

3 tablespoons plain yogurt

freshly ground black pepper

1 celery heart, trimmed and sliced

4 spring onions, trimmed and chopped

125g / 4oz pine nuts, toasted (see page 78)

Pasta in creamy mayonnaise with crisp celery, nuts and apples makes a very pleasant salad. It is very good as part of a group of salads for a buffet.

1 Fill a large saucepan with 4 litres / 7 pints of water and put it on the stove to heat up for the pasta.

2 Meanwhile, put the raisins into a small bowl, cover with boiling water and leave to plump up.

3 When the water in the saucepan boils, add the pasta along with a tablespoon of salt and give the pasta a quick stir. Briefly put the lid on until it starts to lift, showing that the water has come back to the boil, then let the pasta bubble away, uncovered, for about 8 minutes, or until it is tender but still has some bite to it.

4 Cut the apples into small dice or thin slices, removing the core but keeping the skin on. Sprinkle with the lemon juice to preserve the colour.

5 Drain the pasta by tipping it all into a colander placed in the sink, then put it back into the still-warm pan. Add the mayonnaise, yogurt and some salt and pepper to taste and stir gently until all the pasta is coated.

6 Drain the raisins and add to the mixture, along with the apples with their lemon juice, the celery and the spring onions. Check the seasoning, then serve immediately, or cover and leave until the salad cools to room temperature. Either way, scatter with the toasted pine nuts just before serving.

RUOTE DI CARRO WITH SWEETCORN, RED AND GREEN PEPPER AND CHILLI VINAIGRETTE Serves ❹

Fresh raw peppers are used in this recipe, giving a crisp texture and refreshing flavour. They combine well with the sweetcorn, making this a popular salad with children – who might prefer a not too 'hot' version, so just add chilli to taste, or leave it out. Ruote di carro (cartwheel-shaped pasta) is good for this dish, but if you cannot get it, use another smallish pasta such as orecchiette or farfalle.

1 Fill a large saucepan with 4 litres / 7 pints of water and put it on the stove to heat up for the pasta.

2 When the water boils, add the pasta along with a tablespoon of salt and give the pasta a quick stir. Briefly put the lid on until it starts to lift, showing that the water has come back to the boil, then let the pasta bubble away, uncovered, for about 8 minutes, or until it is tender but still has some bite to it.

3 Make a vinaigrette by putting the oil, vinegar, mustard, chilli, garlic and a seasoning of salt and pepper into a jar and shaking until combined.

4 A couple of minutes before the pasta is ready, add the sweetcorn to the pan – it will only take a minute or two to cook.

5 Drain the pasta and sweetcorn by tipping it all into a colander placed in the sink, then put it back into the pan and add the chopped peppers. Give the vinaigrette a quick shake, then add to the pasta and stir gently until everything is coated. Serve immediately, or cover and leave until the salad cools to room temperature.

PENNE SALAD WITH RADICCHIO, RED PEPPER AND BLACK OLIVES Serves ❹

INGREDIENTS

2 red peppers
400g / 14oz penne
salt
3 tablespoons olive oil
1 tablespoon wine vinegar
½ teaspoon Dijon mustard
1 garlic clove, peeled and crushed
freshly ground black pepper
1 small radicchio, shredded or torn
125g / 4oz black olives

This is a lovely salad for autumn, with sweet, succulent grilled red peppers contrasting with bitter-tasting radicchio leaves and salty black olives.

1 Fill a large saucepan with 4 litres / 7 pints of water and put it on the stove to heat up for the pasta.

2 Next prepare the peppers by cutting them into quarters and placing, skin-side (shiny-side) up, on a grill pan. Put under a high heat for 10–15 minutes, until the skin has blistered and blackened in places. Cover the peppers with a plate and leave until cool enough to handle, then remove the skin, stem and seeds, and cut the flesh into strips.

3 When the water in the saucepan boils, add the pasta along with a tablespoon of salt and give the pasta a quick stir. Briefly put the lid on until it starts to lift, showing that the water has come back to the boil, then let the pasta bubble away, uncovered, for about 8 minutes, or until it is tender but still has some bite to it.

4 Make a vinaigrette by putting the oil, vinegar, mustard, garlic and a seasoning of salt and pepper into a jar and shaking until combined.

5 Drain the pasta by tipping it all into a colander placed in the sink, then put it back into the still-warm pan. Add the red pepper strips, radicchio and olives. Give the vinaigrette a quick shake, then add to the pasta and stir gently until everything is coated. Serve immediately, or cover and leave until the salad cools to room temperature.

PENNE RIGATE SALAD WITH BROCCOLI AND CHERRY TOMATOES Serves ❹

INGREDIENTS

400g / 14oz penne rigate

salt

225g / 8oz broccoli, divided into small florets, tough stems removed and tender stems chopped

3 tablespoons olive oil

1 tablespoon wine vinegar

½ teaspoon Dijon mustard

1 garlic clove, peeled and crushed

freshly ground black pepper

225g / 8oz cherry tomatoes, halved

2–3 good sprigs of basil, freshly torn or shredded

The combination of white pasta with green broccoli and red cherry tomatoes makes this a particularly good salad for a Christmas meal, giving a festive look to the table – but it is delicious any time of the year.

1 Fill a large saucepan with 4 litres / 7 pints of water and put it on the stove to heat up for the pasta.

2 When the water boils, add the pasta along with a tablespoon of salt and give the pasta a quick stir. Briefly put the lid on until it starts to lift, showing that the water has come back to the boil, then let the pasta bubble away, uncovered, for about 8 minutes, or until it is tender but still has some bite to it.

3 Meanwhile, cook the broccoli in a little boiling water for 3–4 minutes until tender. Drain the broccoli.

4 Make a vinaigrette by putting the oil, vinegar, mustard, garlic and a seasoning of salt and pepper into a jar and shaking until combined.

5 Drain the pasta by tipping it all into a colander placed in the sink, then put it back into the still-warm pan. Add the broccoli, cherry tomatoes and basil. Give the vinaigrette a quick shake, then add to the pasta and stir gently until everything is coated. Serve immediately, or cover and leave until the salad cools to room temperature.

FUSILLI SALAD WITH COTTAGE CHEESE, CHERRY TOMATOES AND CHIVES IN LEMON VINAIGRETTE Serves ❹

INGREDIENTS

400g / 14oz fusilli

salt

3 tablespoons olive oil

1 tablespoon lemon juice

finely grated or thinly pared rind of ½–1 lemon

½ teaspoon Dijon mustard

1 garlic clove, peeled and crushed

freshly ground black pepper

225g / 8oz cottage cheese

225g / 8oz cherry tomatoes, halved

2 tablespoons freshly chopped chives

A perfect light salad for summer. Use a zester to make the lemon strands if you have one; otherwise grate the lemon rind finely, or peel thinly and then chop into strands.

1 Fill a large saucepan with 4 litres / 7 pints of water and put it on the stove to heat up for the pasta.

2 When the water boils, add the pasta along with a tablespoon of salt and give the pasta a quick stir. Briefly put the lid on until it starts to lift, showing that the water has come back to the boil, then let the pasta bubble away, uncovered, for about 8 minutes, or until it is tender but still has some bite to it.

3 Make a vinaigrette by putting the oil, lemon juice and rind, mustard, garlic and a seasoning of salt and pepper into a jar and shaking until combined.

4 Drain the pasta by tipping it all into a colander placed in the sink, then put it back into the still-warm pan. Add the cottage cheese, breaking it up roughly with a fork so that it is in lumps rather than finely distributed, together with the cherry tomatoes and chives. Give the vinaigrette a quick shake, then add to the pasta and stir gently until everything is coated. Serve immediately, or cover and leave until the salad cools to room temperature.

SALADE NIÇOISE WITH CONCHIGLIE Serves ❹

INGREDIENTS

400g / 14oz conchiglie

salt

3 tablespoons olive oil

1 tablespoon wine vinegar

½ teaspoon Dijon mustard

1 garlic clove, peeled and crushed

freshly ground black pepper

4 tomatoes, preferably plum, roughly chopped

4 hard-boiled eggs, shelled and sliced

bunch of spring onions, trimmed and chopped

50g / 2oz black olives

2 tablespoons freshly chopped or torn flat-leaf parsley

Adding pasta to a vegetarian salade niçoise results in a lovely, substantial mixture which makes an excellent main course.

1 Fill a large saucepan with 4 litres / 7 pints of water and put it on the stove to heat up for the pasta.

2 When the water boils, add the pasta along with a tablespoon of salt and give the pasta a quick stir. Briefly put the lid on until it starts to lift, showing that the water has come back to the boil, then let the pasta bubble away, uncovered, for about 8 minutes, or until it is tender but still has some bite to it.

3 Make a vinaigrette by putting the oil, vinegar, mustard, garlic and a seasoning of salt and pepper into a jar and shaking until combined.

4 Drain the pasta by tipping it all into a colander placed in the sink, then put it back into the still-warm pan. Add the tomatoes, hard-boiled eggs, spring onions, black olives and parsley. Give the vinaigrette a quick shake, then add to the pasta and stir gently until everything is coated. Serve immediately, or cover and leave until the salad cools to room temperature.

GNOCCHI, AVOCADO AND TOMATO SALAD WITH BASIL VINAIGRETTE Serves ❹

INGREDIENTS

400g / 14oz gnocchi

salt

3 tablespoons olive oil

1 tablespoon wine vinegar

½ teaspoon Dijon mustard

1 garlic clove, peeled and crushed

freshly ground black pepper

450g / 1lb tomatoes, sliced

2–3 good sprigs of basil, torn or shredded

1 avocado pear

juice of ½ lemon

This salad can be made in advance and allowed to get cool, but, if you do so, add the avocado at the last moment so that it keeps its bright colour.

1 Fill a large saucepan with 4 litres / 7 pints of water and put it on the stove to heat up for the pasta.

2 When the water boils, add the pasta along with a tablespoon of salt and give the pasta a quick stir. Briefly put the lid on until it starts to lift, showing that the water has come back to the boil, then let the pasta bubble away, uncovered, for about 8 minutes, or until it is tender but still has some bite to it.

3 Make a vinaigrette by putting the oil, vinegar, mustard, garlic and salt and pepper into a jar and shaking until combined.

4 Drain the pasta by tipping it all into a colander placed in the sink, then put it back into the still-warm pan. Give the vinaigrette a quick shake, then add to the pasta and stir gently until the pasta is coated.

5 Allow to cool, then add the tomatoes and basil. Just before serving, halve the avocado, remove the stone and skin, and slice the flesh. Sprinkle with the lemon juice and salt and pepper and add to the salad. Toss the salad gently, then serve as soon as possible.

Salade niçoise with conchiglie

CONCHIGLIE SALAD WITH FENNEL, TOMATOES AND OLIVES Serves ❹

INGREDIENTS

400g / 14oz conchiglie

salt

3 tablespoons olive oil

1 tablespoon wine vinegar

½ teaspoon Dijon mustard

1 garlic clove, peeled and crushed

freshly ground black pepper

1 large fennel

450g / 1lb tomatoes, preferably plum, roughly chopped

125g / 4oz black olives

Fennel, with its crunchy texture and aniseed flavour, makes a refreshing ingredient in this salad but you could use a celery heart instead.

1 Fill a large saucepan with 4 litres / 7 pints of water and put it on the stove to heat up for the pasta.

2 When the water boils, add the pasta along with a tablespoon of salt and give the pasta a quick stir. Briefly put the lid on until it starts to lift, showing that the water has come back to the boil, then let the pasta bubble away, uncovered, for about 8 minutes, or until it is tender but still has some bite to it.

3 Make a vinaigrette by putting the oil, vinegar, mustard, garlic and salt and pepper into a jar and shaking until combined.

4 Cut any leafy bits off the fennel, chop them roughly and leave them on one side. With a sharp knife pare from the fennel any tough, stringy outer layers, then dice or chop the flesh.

5 Drain the pasta by tipping it all into a colander placed in the sink, then put it back into the still-warm pan. Add the fennel, tomatoes and olives. Give the vinaigrette a quick shake, then add to the pasta and stir gently until everything is coated. Scatter the reserved leafy bits of fennel on top. Serve immediately, or cover and leave until the salad cools to room temperature.

FUSILLI SALAD WITH CUCUMBER, DILL MAYONNAISE AND TOASTED ALMONDS Serves ❹

INGREDIENTS

400g / 14oz fusilli

salt

3 tablespoons mayonnaise

3 tablespoons plain yogurt

½ cucumber, cut into 6mm / ¼ inch dice

4 spring onions, trimmed and chopped

2 tablespoons freshly chopped dill

freshly ground black pepper

125g / 4oz flaked almonds, toasted (see page 78)

Like the other salads in this book which contain mayonnaise, this salad is dressed with a mixture of mayonnaise and plain yogurt, for a less fatty result. You could add a greater or smaller quantity of yogurt (or none at all) for a lighter or richer result, according to your taste. In any case, this salad is good with some warm, crusty bread.

1 Fill a large saucepan with 4 litres / 7 pints of water and put it on the stove to heat up for the pasta.

2 When the water boils, add the pasta along with a tablespoon of salt and give the pasta a quick stir. Briefly put the lid on until it starts to lift, showing that the water has come back to the boil, then let the pasta bubble away, uncovered, for about 8 minutes, or until it is tender but still has some bite to it.

3 Drain the pasta by tipping it all into a colander placed in the sink, then put it back into the still-warm pan. Add the mayonnaise, yogurt, cucumber, spring onions, dill and some salt and pepper to taste. Serve immediately, or cover and leave until the salad cools to room temperature. Either way, stir in the toasted flaked almonds just before serving the salad.

CAESAR SALAD WITH FARFALLE Serves ❹

INGREDIENTS

400g / 14oz farfalle

salt

4 thick slices of baguette

olive oil

3 tablespoons mayonnaise

3 tablespoons plain yogurt

½ iceberg lettuce, shredded

4 spring onions, trimmed and chopped

125g / 4oz Parmesan cheese, cut in flakes or coarsely grated

hot chilli sauce, such as Tabasco, to taste

freshly ground black pepper

a little freshly chopped or torn parsley

This Caesar salad, with its creamy mayonnaise dressing and crunchy croûtons, is made more substantial with the addition of pasta. It makes an excellent starter or light main course just as it is, or you could serve another salad, such as a simple tomato one, alongside it.

1 Fill a large saucepan with 4 litres / 7 pints of water and put it on the stove to heat up for the pasta.

2 When the water boils, add the pasta along with a tablespoon of salt and give the pasta a quick stir. Briefly put the lid on until it starts to lift, showing that the water has come back to the boil, then let the pasta bubble away, uncovered, for about 8 minutes, or until it is tender but still has some bite to it.

3 Meanwhile, brush the slices of baguette with a little olive oil on each side and grill on both sides until crisp and golden. Cut into chunky croûtons.

4 Drain the pasta by tipping it all into a colander placed in the sink, then put it back into the still-warm pan. Add the mayonnaise, yogurt, lettuce, spring onions, half the Parmesan, and chilli sauce, salt and pepper to taste, and stir gently until everything is combined.

5 Just before you want to serve the salad, stir in the croûtons and scatter with the parsley and remaining Parmesan.

CONCHIGLIE IN CURRIED MAYONNAISE WITH RAISINS, CELERY, SPRING ONIONS AND CORIANDER Serves ❹

INGREDIENTS

50g / 2oz raisins

400g / 14oz conchiglie

salt

3 tablespoons mayonnaise

3 tablespoons plain yogurt

curry paste to taste

freshly ground black pepper

1 celery heart, trimmed and sliced

4 spring onions, trimmed and chopped

3–4 tablespoons roughly chopped fresh coriander

This is good served with some poppadums for a crisp contrast – or serve it with roasted cashew nuts or peanuts and perhaps mango chutney.

1 Fill a large saucepan with 4 litres / 7 pints of water and put it on the stove to heat up for the pasta.

2 Meanwhile, put the raisins into a small bowl, cover with boiling water and leave to plump up.

3 When the water in the saucepan boils, add the pasta and a tablespoon of salt and give the pasta a stir. Put the lid on until it starts to lift, showing that the water has come back to the boil, then let the pasta bubble away, uncovered, for about 8 minutes, or until it is tender but still has some bite to it.

4 Mix the mayonnaise with the yogurt and add some curry paste to your taste. Season with salt and pepper.

5 Drain the pasta by tipping it all into a colander placed in the sink, then put it back into the pan and add the mayonnaise mixture. Drain the raisins and add them to the mixture, along with the celery and spring onions. Check the seasoning, then serve immediately, or cover and leave until the salad cools to room temperature. Scatter with fresh coriander just before serving.

FUSILLI VINAIGRETTE WITH COURGETTES, AVOCADO AND SUMMER HERBS Serves ❹ as a main course, ❻ to ❽ as a starter

INGREDIENTS

400g / 14oz fusilli

salt

450g / 1lb courgettes, trimmed and cut into 6mm / ¼ inch slices (or matchsticks)

3 tablespoons olive oil

1 tablespoon wine vinegar

½ teaspoon Dijon mustard

1 garlic clove, peeled and crushed

freshly ground black pepper

1 avocado pear

1 tablespoon freshly chopped or torn flat-leaf parsley

1 tablespoon freshly chopped or torn chervil

1 tablespoon freshly chopped chives

Gentle flavours and refreshing colours make this a favourite summer salad. It can be served as a main course, perhaps with some bread and an additional salad (made from plum tomatoes and fresh basil, for example), or served in smaller portions as a starter.

1 Fill a large saucepan with 4 litres / 7 pints of water and put it on the stove to heat up for the pasta.

2 When the water boils, add the pasta along with a tablespoon of salt and give the pasta a quick stir. Briefly put the lid on until it starts to lift, showing that the water has come back to the boil, then let the pasta bubble away, uncovered, for about 8 minutes, or until it is tender but still has some bite to it.

3 Meanwhile, cook the courgettes in a little boiling water for 3–4 minutes until tender. Drain the courgettes.

4 Make a vinaigrette by putting the oil, vinegar, mustard, garlic and a seasoning of salt and pepper into a jar and shaking until combined.

5 Halve the avocado, spear the stone with the tip of a knife and pull it out, then peel off the skin. Slice the flesh.

6 Drain the pasta by tipping it all into a colander placed in the sink, then put it back into the still-warm pan. Add the courgettes, avocado and herbs. Give the vinaigrette a quick shake, then add to the pasta and stir gently until everything is coated. Serve at once, before the avocado loses its bright colour.

ORZI SALAD WITH LEMON, OLIVES AND FRESH HERBS Serves ❹

INGREDIENTS

400g / 14oz orzi

salt

3 tablespoons olive oil

1 tablespoon lemon juice

finely grated or thinly pared rind of ½ lemon

½ teaspoon Dijon mustard

1 garlic clove, peeled and crushed

freshly ground black pepper

50g / 2oz black olives

8 sun-dried tomatoes, chopped

4 tablespoons freshly chopped herbs

Orzi, a fine, small pasta not unlike rice or couscous, makes an excellent base for all kinds of delicious salads. Start with a good vinaigrette and then add salad ingredients to your taste.

1 Fill a large saucepan with 4 litres / 7 pints of water and put it on the stove to heat up for the pasta.

2 When the water boils, add the pasta along with a tablespoon of salt and give the pasta a quick stir. Briefly put the lid on until it starts to lift, showing that the water has come back to the boil, then let the pasta bubble away, uncovered, for about 6 minutes, or until it is tender but still has some bite to it.

3 Make a vinaigrette by putting the oil, lemon juice and rind, mustard, garlic and a seasoning of salt and pepper into a jar and shaking until combined.

4 Drain the pasta by tipping it all into a colander placed in the sink, then put it back into the still-warm pan. Give the vinaigrette a quick shake, then add to the pasta, along with the olives, sun-dried tomatoes and herbs, and stir gently until everything is coated. Serve immediately, or cover and leave until the salad cools to room temperature.

FUSILLI AND CHICKPEA SALAD WITH SPRING ONIONS Serves ❹

INGREDIENTS

400g / 14oz fusilli

salt

3 tablespoons olive oil

1 tablespoon wine vinegar

1 garlic clove, peeled and crushed

freshly ground black pepper

a 400g/14oz can chickpeas, drained

bunch of spring onions, trimmed and chopped

150ml / 5fl oz crème fraîche, optional

This simple salad is good served with an interesting bread such as walnut or sun-dried tomato. The crème fraîche is optional, but delicious for a treat.

1 Fill a large saucepan with 4 litres / 7 pints of water and put it on the stove to heat up for the pasta.

2 When the water boils, add the pasta along with a tablespoon of salt and give the pasta a quick stir. Briefly put the lid on until it starts to lift, showing that the water has come back to the boil, then let the pasta bubble away, uncovered, for about 8 minutes, or until it is tender but still has some bite to it.

3 Make a vinaigrette by putting the oil, vinegar, garlic and a seasoning of salt and pepper into a jar and shaking until combined.

4 Drain the pasta by tipping it all into a colander placed in the sink, then put it back into the still-warm pan. Add the chickpeas and spring onions. Give the vinaigrette a quick shake, then add to the pasta and stir gently until everything is coated. Serve immediately, or cover and leave until the salad cools to room temperature. Either way, offer the crème fraîche separately, if using.

PASTA AND BEAN SALAD WITH CHILLI-TOMATO VINAIGRETTE Serves ❹

INGREDIENTS

400g / 14oz any chunky pasta, such as farfalle, fusilli, conchiglie or penne

salt

3 tablespoons olive oil

1 tablespoon wine vinegar

1 tablespoon sun-dried tomato purée

1 garlic clove, peeled and crushed

hot chilli sauce, such as Tabasco, to taste

freshly ground black pepper

a 420g / 15oz can red kidney beans, drained

1 mild onion, peeled and sliced

1 green pepper, de-seeded and finely chopped

2 tablespoons freshly chopped coriander or parsley

Pasta and beans make a great combination: a filling and satisfactory main course if you serve them with some fresh leafy salad. You can add almost anything to the bean salad — trust your inspiration and the contents of your storecupboard and fridge. You could use other types of canned beans such as cannellini beans, black-eyed beans, flageolets or even green lentils instead of the red kidney beans. Some grated carrot and/or sliced avocado is also good in this salad.

1 Fill a large saucepan with 4 litres / 7 pints of water and put it on the stove to heat up for the pasta.

2 When the water boils, add the pasta along with a tablespoon of salt and give the pasta a quick stir. Briefly put the lid on until it starts to lift, showing that the water has come back to the boil, then let the pasta bubble away, uncovered, for about 8 minutes, or until it is tender but still has some bite to it.

3 Make a vinaigrette by putting the oil, vinegar, sun-dried tomato purée, garlic, chilli sauce to your taste and a seasoning of salt and pepper into a jar and shaking until combined.

4 Drain the pasta by tipping it all into a colander placed in the sink, then put it back into the still-warm pan. Add the beans, onion and green pepper. Give the vinaigrette a quick shake, then add to the pasta, along with the chopped herbs, and stir gently until everything is coated. Serve immediately, or cover and leave until the salad cools to room temperature.

Five-minute Sauces

This section is in the book at the request of my daughter Meg, a busy doctor who has little time for cooking during the week. As the name suggests, all the sauces or additions to the pasta can be prepared in five minutes, while the pasta cooks. Each dish can stand alone as a complete main course, although I like to serve them with a green or mixed salad on the side, and bread for those who want it.

Some of the dishes only need storecupboard ingredients, and so are ideal for those times when you need to make a meal quickly and have had no time to shop. If you keep a few standby ingredients in the cupboard, along with pasta and olive oil, you will never be stuck for a quick meal. Good basics to keep in are: sun-dried tomatoes and sun-dried tomato purée, dried red chillies, dried porcini mushrooms, good quality olive oil (of course), garlic, and black olives. I do not use cans much besides these two: canned plum tomatoes and artichoke hearts, both of which are useful and good to have at hand. In the freezer it is useful to keep a packet of frozen peas (I like petit pois), and one of sweetcorn kernels. Some pine nuts and any other type of nut that you like, such as walnuts and pecans, are useful to have in, and best kept in the refrigerator or freezer if you have room. If you like Parmesan cheese, keep a piece of that in the refrigerator, too.

PENNE WITH VODKA AND PEAS Serves ❹

INGREDIENTS

400g / 14oz penne

salt

225g / 8oz podded fresh peas or frozen petits pois

1 tablespoon olive oil

8 tablespoons vodka

freshly ground black pepper

With vodka added at the last minute, this dish definitely has an alcoholic kick to it. If you prefer, you can boil off the alcohol: simply allow the vodka to come briefly to the boil in the pasta pan.

1 Fill a large saucepan with 4 litres / 7 pints of water and put it on the stove to heat up for the pasta.

2 When the water boils, add the pasta along with a tablespoon of salt and give the pasta a quick stir. Briefly put the lid on until it starts to lift, showing that the water has come back to the boil, then let the pasta bubble away, uncovered, for about 8 minutes, or until it is tender but still has some bite to it.

3 Just before the pasta is done, add the peas to it and cook briefly, just to heat the peas through.

4 Drain the pasta and peas by tipping them into a colander placed in the sink, then put them back into the still-warm pan, add the olive oil, vodka and a grinding of black pepper, and serve onto warm plates.

FARFALLE WITH SHIITAKE MUSHROOMS, PARMESAN AND SAGE Serves ❹

INGREDIENTS

400g / 14oz farfalle

salt

450g / 1lb fresh shiitake mushrooms, washed and sliced

2 tablespoons olive oil

1 garlic clove, peeled and crushed

6 fresh sage leaves, chopped

freshly ground black pepper

50g / 2oz freshly flaked Parmesan cheese

Fresh shiitake mushrooms are good in this; otherwise try chestnut mushrooms.

1 Fill a large saucepan with 4 litres / 7 pints of water and put it on the stove to heat up for the pasta.

2 When the water boils, add the pasta along with a tablespoon of salt and give the pasta a quick stir. Briefly put the lid on until it starts to lift, showing that the water has come back to the boil, then let the pasta bubble away, uncovered, for about 8 minutes, or until it is tender but still has some bite to it.

3 Meanwhile, fry the mushrooms in the olive oil, with the garlic, for 4–5 minutes, until tender and any liquid has boiled away. Stir in the sage and season with salt and pepper.

4 Drain the pasta by tipping it all into a colander placed in the sink, then put it back into the still-warm pan, add the mushroom and sage mixture and Parmesan, and serve onto warm plates.

PENNE WITH SPINACH, MASCARPONE AND PARMESAN Serves ❹

INGREDIENTS

400g / 14oz penne

salt

125g / 4oz mascarpone cheese, or reduced-fat cream cheese

450g / 1lb baby spinach leaves, washed and shredded

freshly ground black pepper

fresh Parmesan cheese, cut in flakes or grated, to serve

A lovely, simple pasta dish which makes the most of the flavour of tender spinach leaves. As with the other mascarpone recipes in this book, you can substitute a reduced-fat cream cheese to save some calories if you wish.

1 Fill a large saucepan with 4 litres / 7 pints of water and put it on the stove to heat up for the pasta.

2 When the water boils, add the pasta along with a tablespoon of salt and give the pasta a quick stir. Briefly put the lid on until it starts to lift, showing that the water has come back to the boil, then let the pasta bubble away, uncovered, for about 8 minutes, or until it is tender but still has some bite to it.

3 Drain the pasta by tipping it all into a colander placed in the sink, then put it back into the still-warm pan with the mascarpone cheese and stir gently until the cheese has heated through but not boiled. Add the shredded spinach, which will cook in the heat of the pasta, mix gently, season with salt and pepper and serve immediately onto warm plates with the Parmesan on top.

FARFALLE WITH MANGETOUT, LEMON AND BASIL Serves ❹ as a main course, ❻ to ❽ as a starter

INGREDIENTS

400g / 14oz farfalle

salt

350g / 12oz mangetout, trimmed

2 tablespoons olive oil

finely grated or thinly pared rind of 1 lemon

juice of 1 lemon

freshly ground black pepper

4 good sprigs of fresh basil leaves

Nice and simple and fresh-tasting, this is good served either as a starter or as a light summer dish.

1 Fill a large saucepan with 4 litres / 7 pints of water and put it on the stove to heat up for the pasta.

2 When the water boils, add the pasta along with a tablespoon of salt and give the pasta a quick stir. Briefly put the lid on until it starts to lift, showing that the water has come back to the boil, then let the pasta bubble away, uncovered, for about 8 minutes, or until it is tender but still has some bite to it.

3 Just before the pasta is done, add the mangetout to it and cook briefly, just to heat through.

4 Drain the pasta and mangetout by tipping them into a colander placed in the sink, then put them back into the still-warm pan, add the olive oil, lemon rind and juice and a grinding of black pepper, and serve onto warm plates. Tear the basil over the top.

LASAGNETTE WITH SUN-DRIED TOMATOES, GARLIC AND BASIL Serves ❹

INGREDIENTS

400g / 14oz lasagnette

salt

2 garlic cloves, peeled and crushed

1 tablespoon olive oil

4 tablespoons sun-dried tomato purée or chopped sun-dried tomatoes

freshly ground black pepper

fresh basil leaves and flakes of Parmesan cheese, to serve

Ultra quick and very good, this recipe makes the most of the intense, rich flavour of sun-dried tomatoes.

1 Fill a large saucepan with 4 litres / 7 pints of water and put it on the stove to heat up for the pasta.

2 When the water boils, add the pasta along with a tablespoon of salt and give the pasta a quick stir. Briefly put the lid on until it starts to lift, showing that the water has come back to the boil, then let the pasta bubble away, uncovered, for about 8 minutes, or until it is tender but still has some bite to it.

3 Just before the pasta is done, cook the garlic in the olive oil over a gentle heat for 2–3 minutes, without letting it brown.

4 Drain the pasta by tipping it all into a colander placed in the sink, then put it back into the still-warm pan, pour in the garlic and its oil and add the sun-dried tomato purée or chopped sun-dried tomatoes and some pepper. Stir gently, then serve onto warm plates. Tear the basil over and scatter the Parmesan on top.

SPAGHETTI WITH GARLIC AND OLIVE OIL Serves ❹

INGREDIENTS

400g / 14oz spaghetti

salt

2–4 fat juicy garlic cloves, peeled and sliced, chopped or crushed

2–4 tablespoons olive oil

freshly ground black pepper

freshly grated Parmesan cheese, to serve, optional

This is the simplest pasta dish in the world. The better the ingredients, the better this dish will be. The garlic can be chopped, crushed or sliced – I prefer it sliced. The amount of oil you add to this recipe is up to you; I do not like it too oily, but you need enough in this recipe to give flavour and moistness to the dish.

1 Fill a large saucepan with 4 litres / 7 pints of water and put it on the stove to heat up for the pasta.

2 When the water boils, add the spaghetti, holding it straight up like a bunch of flowers and gently pushing it into the water as it softens. Add a tablespoon of salt and give the pasta a quick stir. Briefly put the lid on until it starts to lift, showing that the water has come back to the boil, then let the pasta bubble away, uncovered, for about 8 minutes, or until it is tender but still has some bite to it.

.3 Meanwhile, cook the garlic in the olive oil over a gentle heat – it needs just to soften and warm through without going brown.

4 Drain the pasta by tipping it all into a colander placed in the sink, then put it back into the still-warm pan, add the garlic and its oil along with a good grinding of salt and pepper as needed, toss gently and serve onto warm plates. Hand round the Parmesan, if desired.

SPAGHETTI WITH OLIVE OIL AND RED CHILLI FLAKES Serves ❹

INGREDIENTS

400g / 14oz spaghetti

salt

2 garlic cloves, peeled and finely chopped

2–4 tablespoons olive oil

1–2 dried red chillies, crumbled

freshly ground black pepper

fresh Parmesan cheese, cut in flakes or grated, to serve, optional

torn or chopped fresh flat-leaf parsley, to serve, optional

So simple to make, yet so good, in this recipe the amounts of chilli, garlic and olive oil can be varied to suit your taste. Little dried red chillies (which you can buy at any supermarket) are very hot, so go carefully.

1 Fill a large saucepan with 4 litres / 7 pints of water and put it on the stove to heat up for the pasta.

2 When the water in the saucepan boils, add the spaghetti, holding it straight up like a bunch of flowers and gently pushing it into the water as it softens. Add a tablespoon of salt and give the pasta a quick stir. Briefly put the lid on until it starts to lift, showing that the water has come back to the boil, then let the pasta bubble away, uncovered, for about 8 minutes, or until it is tender but still has some bite to it.

3 Just before the pasta is done, cook the garlic in the olive oil over a gentle heat for 2–3 minutes without letting it brown. Then add the chilli – stand back, as the oil released by chilli on contact with heat can make you cough – and stir-fry for a few seconds. Leave on one side until the spaghetti is done.

4 Drain the pasta by tipping it all into a colander placed in the sink, then put it back into the still-warm pan. Quickly reheat the garlic mixture, then pour it onto the pasta. Stir gently, season with salt and pepper as necessary, then serve it onto warm plates and top with some Parmesan and/or parsley, according to your taste.

FUSILLI WITH GARLIC AND HERB CREAM CHEESE AND YOUNG PEAS Serves ❹

INGREDIENTS

400g / 14oz fusilli

salt

225g / 8oz podded fresh young peas or frozen petits pois

150g / 5oz garlic and herb cream cheese, full fat or reduced fat

Fresh peas are delicious in this if you can get them; otherwise, frozen petits pois make a good substitute.

1 Fill a large saucepan with 4 litres / 7 pints of water and put it on the stove to heat up for the pasta.

2 When the water in the saucepan boils, add the pasta along with a tablespoon of salt and give the pasta a quick stir. Briefly put the lid on until it starts to lift, showing that the water has come back to the boil, then let

the pasta bubble away, uncovered, for about 8 minutes, or until it is tender but still has some bite to it.

3 Just before the pasta is done, add the peas to it and cook briefly, just to heat the peas through.

4 Drain the pasta and peas by tipping them into a colander placed in the sink, then put them back into the still-warm pan with the cream cheese, toss gently and serve onto warm plates.

GNOCCHI WITH MUSHROOMS, ARTICHOKES, MASCARPONE AND FRESH BASIL Serves ❹

INGREDIENTS

400g / 14oz gnocchi

salt

350g / 12oz mushrooms, washed and sliced

1 tablespoon olive oil

1 garlic clove, peeled and crushed

a 400g / 14oz can artichoke hearts, drained and sliced

125g / 4oz mascarpone cheese, or reduced-fat cream cheese

freshly ground black pepper

fresh basil leaves, to serve

Serve this creamy pasta dish with some crisp garlic bread. Mascarpone is luscious but high in calories; for a less rich dish, use a reduced-fat cream cheese instead.

1 Fill a large saucepan with 4 litres / 7 pints of water and put it on the stove to heat up for the pasta.

2 When the water boils, add the pasta along with a tablespoon of salt and give the pasta a quick stir. Briefly put the lid on until it starts to lift, showing that the water has come back to the boil, then let the pasta bubble away, uncovered, for about 8 minutes, or until it is tender but still has some bite to it.

3 Fry the mushrooms in the olive oil, with the garlic, for 4–5 minutes, until tender and any liquid has boiled away. Add the artichoke hearts and continue to cook gently until they are heated through.

4 Drain the pasta by tipping it all into a colander placed in the sink, then put it back into the still-warm pan with the mascarpone cheese and stir gently until the cheese has heated through but not boiled. Add the mushroom and artichoke mixture, mix gently and season with salt and pepper. Serve immediately onto warm plates with a generous amount of fresh basil torn or snipped over the top.

FARFALLE WITH MUSHROOMS, PEAS AND PARSLEY Serves ❹

INGREDIENTS

400g / 14oz farfalle

salt

350g / 12oz mushrooms, washed and sliced

25g / 1oz butter

1 tablespoon olive oil

1 garlic clove, peeled and crushed

225g / 8oz podded fresh peas, frozen petits pois or trimmed mangetout

2 tablespoons chopped fresh parsley, flat-leaf if available, to serve

Ordinary mushrooms are fine for this, as are frozen petits pois, although if you can get fresh peas, or mangetout, they would be even better.

1 Fill a large saucepan with 4 litres / 7 pints of water and put it on the stove to heat up for the pasta.

2 When the water boils, add the pasta along with a tablespoon of salt and give the pasta a quick stir. Briefly put the lid on until it starts to lift, showing that the water has come back to the boil, then let the pasta bubble away, uncovered, for about 8 minutes, or until it is tender but still has some bite to it.

3 Fry the mushrooms in the butter and olive oil, with the garlic, for 4–5 minutes, until tender and any liquid has boiled away.

4 Just before the pasta is done, add the peas (or mangetout) to it and cook briefly, just to heat them through.

5 Drain the pasta and peas by tipping them into a colander placed in the sink, then put them back into the still-warm pan, add the mushrooms, toss gently and serve onto warm plates with the parsley on top.

TAGLIATELLE, STILTON AND PECAN NUTS Serves ❹

INGREDIENTS

400g / 14oz tagliatelle, plain or verde

salt

8 tablespoons single cream or pasta cooking water

1 garlic clove, peeled and crushed

175g / 6oz Stilton cheese

freshly ground black pepper

50g / 2oz pecan nuts, roughly chopped, toasted (see page 78)

This recipe was invented by my daughter, Meg. Other blue cheeses can be substituted for the Stilton, and a mixed salad makes a good accompaniment. For a lower-fat version, you can use some of the pasta cooking water instead of the single cream for melting the cheese.

1 Fill a large saucepan with 4 litres / 7 pints of water and put it on the stove to heat up for the pasta.

2 When the water boils, add the pasta along with a tablespoon of salt and give the pasta a quick stir. Briefly put the lid on until it starts to lift, showing that the water has come back to the boil, then let the pasta bubble away, uncovered, for about 8 minutes, or until it is tender but still has some bite to it.

3 Just before the pasta is ready, heat the cream (or the same quantity of water, scooped from the pasta pan) in a small saucepan, add the garlic and crumble in the Stilton cheese. Stir over a gentle heat until the cheese has melted and combined with the liquid to make a creamy sauce – do not let it overheat.

4 Drain the pasta by tipping it all into a colander placed in the sink, then put it back into the still-warm pan and add the cheese mixture. Grind black pepper over, toss gently and serve onto warm plates, scattered with the pecan nuts.

MACARONI, CHEDDAR CHEESE AND CHERRY TOMATOES Serves ❹

INGREDIENTS

400g / 14oz macaroni

salt

1 tablespoon olive oil

350g / 12oz cherry tomatoes, halved

175g / 6oz Cheddar cheese, coarsely grated or cut into small dice

Simple, fresh and pretty to look at, this dish appeals particularly to children.

1 Fill a large saucepan with 4 litres / 7 pints of water and put it on the stove to heat up for the pasta.

2 When the water boils, add the pasta along with a tablespoon of salt and give the pasta a quick stir. Briefly put the lid on until it starts to lift, showing that the water has come back to the boil, then let the pasta bubble away, uncovered, for about 8 minutes, or until it is tender but still has some bite to it.

3 Drain the pasta by tipping it all into a colander placed in the sink, then put it back into the still-warm pan, add the olive oil and toss gently before adding the tomatoes and cheese. Mix again, to combine, then serve onto warm plates.

FETTUCCINE WITH PEAS, GRUYÈRE AND CREAM Serves ❹

INGREDIENTS

400g / 14oz fettuccine

salt

150ml / 5fl oz single cream

125g / 4oz Gruyère cheese, grated

225g / 8oz fresh podded peas or frozen petits pois

In this recipe, the cheese is melted in the cream to make a sauce which is then mixed with the pasta and peas. It is rich, so serve it with a simple tomato or leafy salad to provide the perfect balance.

1 Fill a large saucepan with 4 litres / 7 pints of water and put it on the stove to heat up for the pasta.

2 When the water boils, add the pasta along with a tablespoon of salt and give the pasta a quick stir. Briefly put the lid on until it starts to lift, showing that the water has come back to the boil, then let the pasta bubble away, uncovered, for about 8 minutes, or until it is tender but still has some bite to it.

3 Meanwhile, heat the cream and cheese in a small saucepan over a gentle heat until the cheese has melted, then remove from the heat.

4 Just before the pasta is done, add the peas to it and cook briefly, just to heat the peas through. Quickly reheat the cheese mixture, but do not let it boil.

5 Drain the pasta and peas by tipping them into a colander placed in the sink, then put them back into the still-warm pan, add the cheese mixture, toss gently and serve onto warm plates.

FETTUCCINE WITH SUN-DRIED TOMATOES, GARLIC AND BASIL Serves ❹

INGREDIENTS

400g / 14oz fettuccine

salt

2–4 fat juicy garlic cloves, peeled and sliced

2–4 tablespoons olive oil or oil from the sun-dried tomatoes

12 sun-dried tomatoes, chopped

freshly ground black pepper

fresh basil leaves and flakes of Parmesan cheese, to serve

I love the intense flavour of sun-dried tomatoes. For texture and appearance in this recipe I use whole ones which I slice, but you could equally well use sun-dried tomato purée if you prefer.

1 Fill a large saucepan with 4 litres / 7 pints of water and put it on the stove to heat up for the pasta.

2 When the water boils, add the pasta along with a tablespoon of salt and give the pasta a quick stir. Briefly put the lid on until it starts to lift, showing that the water has come back to the boil, then let the pasta bubble away, uncovered, for about 8 minutes, or until it is tender but still has some bite to it.

3 Meanwhile, cook the garlic in the olive or sun-dried-tomato oil over a gentle heat – it needs just to soften and warm through without going brown. Just before the pasta is done, add the sun-dried tomatoes to the garlic mixture and warm them through over the heat, too.

4 Drain the pasta by tipping it all into a colander placed in the sink, then put it back into the still-warm pan, add the garlic mixture and salt and pepper to taste, toss gently and serve onto warm plates. Tear the basil over and scatter the Parmesan on top.

PENNONI WITH AVOCADO, CHILLI AND CORIANDER Serves ❹

INGREDIENTS

400g / 14oz pennoni

salt

1 garlic clove, peeled and crushed

1 fresh green chilli, de-seeded and finely sliced

1 tablespoon olive oil

1 avocado pear, peeled and sliced

juice of 1 lemon

freshly ground black pepper

4 tablespoons roughly chopped fresh coriander, to serve

We do not often think of avocado in terms of a hot pasta dish, but this is a combination I like. It is important not to let the avocado get too hot or the flavour will be spoilt. Some crunchy garlic bread goes well with this dish, and maybe a tomato salad too.

1 Fill a large saucepan with 4 litres / 7 pints of water and put it on the stove to heat up for the pasta.

2 When the water boils, add the pasta along with a tablespoon of salt and give the pasta a quick stir. Briefly put the lid on until it starts to lift, showing that the water has come back to the boil, then let the pasta bubble away, uncovered, for about 8 minutes, or until it is tender but still has some bite to it.

3 Meanwhile, cook the garlic and chilli in the olive oil over a gentle heat for 2–3 minutes, until softened but not browned. Keep on one side.

4 Toss the avocado in the lemon juice and season with salt and pepper.

5 Drain the pasta by tipping it all into a colander placed in the sink, then put it back into the still-warm pan and add the chilli mixture and avocado. Toss gently and serve onto warm plates, with the coriander on top.

TAGLIATELLE WITH GREEN PEPPERCORNS Serves ❹

INGREDIENTS

400g / 14oz tagliatelle

salt

2–4 tablespoons olive oil

1 tablespoon green peppercorns

freshly ground black pepper

freshly chopped parsley or chervil, to serve

freshly grated Parmesan or pecorino cheese, to serve

Piquant green peppercorns make a pleasant contrast with bland pasta. This is also good made with spaghetti or one of the short pastas, such as penne, if you prefer.

1 Fill a large saucepan with 4 litres / 7 pints of water and put it on the stove to heat up for the pasta.

2 When the water boils, add the pasta along with a tablespoon of salt and give the pasta a quick stir. Briefly put the lid on until it starts to lift, showing that the water has come back to the boil, then let the pasta bubble away, uncovered, for about 8 minutes, or until it is tender but still has some bite to it.

3 Drain the pasta by tipping it all into a colander placed in the sink, then put it back into the still-warm pan, add the olive oil, green peppercorns and salt and black pepper to taste, toss gently and serve onto warm plates, with herbs and cheese scattered over the top.

FETTUCCINE WITH LEMON Serves ❹

INGREDIENTS

400g / 14oz fettuccine

salt

1 fat juicy garlic clove, peeled and crushed

2–4 tablespoons olive oil

finely grated or thinly pared rind of 1 lemon

juice of 1 lemon

freshly ground black pepper

freshly torn flat-leaf parsley, to serve, optional

freshly grated Parmesan cheese, to serve, optional

This is a delicate combination of flavours. If you have a zester, and can make thin strands of lemon rind, they look particularly pretty with the fettuccine.

1 Fill a large saucepan with 4 litres / 7 pints of water and put it on the stove to heat up for the pasta.

2 When the water boils, add the pasta along with a tablespoon of salt and give the pasta a quick stir. Briefly put the lid on until it starts to lift, showing that the water has come back to the boil, then let the pasta bubble away, uncovered, for about 8 minutes, or until it is tender but still has some bite to it.

3 Meanwhile, cook the garlic in the olive oil over a gentle heat for 2–3 minutes, without letting it brown. Keep on one side.

4 Drain the pasta by tipping it all into a colander placed in the sink, then put it back into the still-warm pan. Add the garlic and its oil, the lemon rind and juice, and plenty of black pepper. Toss gently, then serve onto warm plates with parsley and Parmesan on top if using.

....

TAGLIATELLE WITH WALNUTS AND WALNUT OIL Serves ❹

INGREDIENTS

400g / 14oz tagliatelle

salt

1 garlic clove, peeled and crushed

1 tablespoon olive oil

2 tablespoons walnut oil

125–175g / 4–6oz shelled walnuts (preferably freshly cracked), roughly chopped

freshly ground black pepper

freshly chopped parsley, to serve, optional

fresh Parmesan cheese, cut in flakes or grated, to serve, optional

This is nicest when made with freshly cracked walnuts — it is well worth the trouble if you have the patience.

1 Fill a large saucepan with 4 litres / 7 pints of water and put it on the stove to heat up for the pasta.

2 When the water boils, add the pasta along with a tablespoon of salt and give the pasta a quick stir. Briefly put the lid on until it starts to lift, showing that the water has come back to the boil, then let the pasta bubble away, uncovered, for about 8 minutes, or until it is tender but still has some bite to it.

3 Meanwhile, cook the garlic in the olive oil over a gentle heat for 2–3 minutes, without letting it brown. Keep on one side.

4 Drain the pasta by tipping it all into a colander placed in the sink, then put it back into the still-warm pan. Add the olive oil and garlic mixture, the walnut oil and walnuts, and grind over black pepper to taste. Toss gently, then serve onto warm plates, with parsley and Parmesan on top if using.

FETTUCCINE WITH RADICCHIO AND PINK PEPPERCORNS Serves ❹

400g / 14oz fettuccine

salt

olive oil

1 radicchio, finely shredded

freshly ground black pepper

1 tablespoon pink peppercorns, lightly crushed

A salad of mixed leaves, including some radicchio and lamb's lettuce, with a light dressing, goes well with this.

1 Fill a large saucepan with 4 litres / 7 pints of water and put it on the stove to heat up for the pasta.

2 When the water boils, add the pasta along with a tablespoon of salt and give the pasta a quick stir. Briefly put the lid on until it starts to lift, showing that the water has come back to the boil, then let the pasta bubble away, uncovered, for about 8 minutes, or until it is tender but still has some bite to it.

3 Just before the pasta is done, heat 2 tablespoons of olive oil in a saucepan and stir-fry the radicchio for 1–2 minutes, until wilted.

4 Drain the pasta by tipping it all into a colander placed in the sink, then put it back into the still-warm pan. Quickly reheat the radicchio, then tip it into the pasta, including the oil, and stir the pasta gently. Add a little extra olive oil if desired, then season with black pepper. Serve the pasta onto warm plates and scatter the pink peppercorns on top.

FUSILLI LUNGHI WITH SPINACH, PINE NUTS AND RAISINS Serves ❹

400g / 14oz fusilli lunghi

salt

2 tablespoons olive oil

450g / 1lb tender spinach leaves, washed

50g / 2oz raisins

freshly ground black pepper

50g / 2oz pine nuts, toasted (see page 78)

Spinach, pine nuts and raisins is a classic combination in Catalan cookery, and one that I love.

1 Fill a large saucepan with 4 litres / 7 pints of water and put it on the stove to heat up for the pasta.

2 When the water boils, add the pasta along with a tablespoon of salt and give the pasta a quick stir. Briefly put the lid on until it starts to lift, showing that the water has come back to the boil, then let the pasta bubble away, uncovered, for about 8 minutes, or until it is tender but still has some bite to it.

3 Meanwhile, heat the olive oil in a large pan and put in the spinach. Stir-fry over a high heat for 2–3 minutes until wilted, then add the raisins and season with salt and pepper.

4 Drain the pasta by tipping it all into a colander placed in the sink, then put it back into the still-warm pan, add the spinach mixture and the pine nuts and toss gently. Serve onto warm plates.

FETTUCCINE IN THE SOUTHERN ITALIAN STYLE WITH ROCKET AND DILL Serves ❹

INGREDIENTS

400g / 14oz fettuccine

salt

2–4 fat juicy garlic cloves, peeled and chopped or thinly sliced

4 tablespoons olive oil

225g / 8oz rocket, chopped

4 good sprigs of dill, chopped

freshly ground black pepper

freshly chopped parsley or chervil, to serve

freshly grated or flaked pecorino cheese, to serve, optional

You really need a substantial bunch of rocket to make this – those little supermarket packets do not contain enough and cost too much to make it worthwhile. The best place to find bunches of rocket is often a Middle-eastern store.

1 Fill a large saucepan with 4 litres / 7 pints of water and put it on the stove to heat up for the pasta.

2 When the water boils, add the pasta along with a tablespoon of salt and give the pasta a quick stir. Briefly put the lid on until it starts to lift, showing that the water has come back to the boil, then let the pasta bubble away, uncovered, for about 8 minutes, or until it is tender but still has some bite to it.

3 Meanwhile, cook the garlic in the olive oil over a gentle heat for 2–3 minutes, without letting it brown. Keep on one side.

4 Drain the pasta by tipping it all into a colander placed in the sink, then put it back into the still-warm pan. Add the garlic and oil, then throw in the rocket and dill, toss gently over the heat so that they warm through briefly, and grind in black pepper to taste. Serve onto warm plates, scatter with parsley and chervil and hand round the pecorino cheese if using.

LUMACHE WITH WILD MUSHROOMS Serves ❹

INGREDIENTS

400g / 14oz lumache

salt

450–700g / 1–1½lb wild mushrooms, washed and sliced as necessary

2 tablespoons olive oil

2 garlic cloves, peeled and crushed

squeeze of lemon juice

freshly ground black pepper

roughly chopped fresh parsley, preferably flat-leaf, to serve, optional

fresh Parmesan cheese, cut in flakes or grated, to serve, optional

You can use any mixture of wild mushrooms for this – or even ordinary ones with just a few more interesting ones added. It is a wonderful combination – the more mushrooms, the better.

1 Fill a large saucepan with 4 litres / 7 pints of water and put it on the stove to heat up for the pasta.

2 When the water boils, add the pasta along with a tablespoon of salt and give the pasta a quick stir. Briefly put the lid on until it starts to lift, showing that the water has come back to the boil, then let the pasta bubble away, uncovered, for about 8 minutes, or until it is tender but still has some bite to it.

3 Meanwhile, fry the mushrooms in the olive oil, with the garlic, for 4–5 minutes, until tender and any liquid has boiled away. Add a squeeze of lemon juice to bring out the flavour, then season with salt and pepper.

4 Drain the pasta by tipping it all into a colander placed in the sink, then put it back into the still-warm pan, add the mushrooms, toss gently and check the seasoning, adding more salt and pepper if necessary. Serve onto warm plates, and scatter the parsley and Parmesan over the top if using.

PENNE WITH ROCKET, PINE NUTS AND PARMESAN Serves ❹

INGREDIENTS

400g / 14oz penne

salt

225g / 8oz rocket

2 garlic cloves, peeled and finely sliced or chopped

olive oil

freshly ground black pepper

squeeze of lemon juice

50g / 2oz pine nuts, toasted (see page 78)

50g / 2oz freshly grated or flaked Parmesan cheese

If you can buy rocket by the bunch it will be much cheaper and you will be able to use it with abandon. It is also very easy to grow, though it can go to seed so you need to keep sowing it throughout the summer.

1 Fill a large saucepan with 4 litres / 7 pints of water and put it on the stove to heat up for the pasta.

2 When the water boils, add the pasta along with a tablespoon of salt and give the pasta a quick stir. Briefly put the lid on until it starts to lift, showing that the water has come back to the boil, then let the pasta bubble away, uncovered, for about 8 minutes, or until it is tender but still has some bite to it.

3 Just before the pasta is done, stir-fry the rocket with the garlic in 2 tablespoons of olive oil for 2–3 minutes, until the rocket is wilted. Season with salt, pepper and a squeeze of lemon juice.

4 Drain the pasta by tipping it all into a colander placed in the sink, then put it back into the still-warm pan. Quickly reheat the rocket, then add it to the pasta, along with a little extra olive oil if you think the mixture needs it, and the pine nuts and Parmesan. Toss gently, check the seasoning, then serve onto warm plates.

FETTUCCINE WITH BUTTER AND DOLCELATTE Serves ❹

INGREDIENTS

400g / 14oz fettuccine

salt

50g / 2oz butter

175g / 6oz dolcelatte cheese

freshly ground black pepper

The sauce is rich but full of flavour so a little goes a long way. If you cannot get dolcelatte cheese, use Gorgonzola or another blue cheese such as Danish blue. A leafy salad, including some hot leaves such as rocket or watercress, goes well with this.

1 Fill a large saucepan with 4 litres / 7 pints of water and put it on the stove to heat up for the pasta.

2 When the water boils, add the pasta along with a tablespoon of salt and give the pasta a quick stir. Briefly put the lid on until it starts to lift, showing that the water has come back to the boil, then let the pasta bubble away, uncovered, for about 8 minutes, or until it is tender but still has some bite to it.

3 Just before the pasta is ready, melt the butter in a small saucepan, crumble in the cheese and stir over a gentle heat until it has melted and combined with the butter to make a creamy sauce – do not let it overheat.

4 Drain the pasta by tipping it all into a colander placed in the sink, then put it back into the still-warm pan and add the cheese mixture. Grind black pepper over, toss gently and serve onto warm plates.

Simple Pasta Dishes

*T*hese take a little longer to make than the Five-minute Sauces but they are still pretty quick and some of them, such as Lumache with feta cheese and broccoli, and Pipe rigate with Swiss chard, mascarpone and pine nuts, take less than ten minutes.

Other recipes which take longer can often be partly prepared in advance then quickly assembled at the last minute. For instance, if you want to make Penne with roasted Mediterranean vegetables, you could roast the vegetables earlier in the day, or even the day before, and keep them covered and cool, ready for later. Even Pennoni with croûtons and caramelized onions could be partially prepared in advance: although the onions take half an hour to cook, they will not spoil if you leave them for a few hours then reheat them just before you serve the pasta.

As with all the recipes in this book, I have specified the type of pasta which I think goes best with the ingredients in the recipe. If you do not agree, or do not have that particular pasta available, by all means make changes and substitutions. Enjoy the recipes and make them your own.

Soy sauce is used in one or two of the recipes in this section, and in other recipes in the book. It is worth seeking out a good soy sauce, properly fermented and made just from soya beans and water without additions such as caramel. Look for a Chinese or Japanese make; a health shop will have them, as will a large supermarket.

ORECCHIETTE WITH OYSTER MUSHROOMS, LEEKS AND SUN-DRIED TOMATOES Serves ❹

INGREDIENTS

225g / 8oz leeks, trimmed and cut into 6mm / ¼ inch slices

2 tablespoons olive oil, or oil from the sun-dried tomatoes (see below)

400g / 14oz orecchiette

salt

225g / 8oz oyster mushrooms, washed and sliced

8 sun-dried tomatoes, chopped

freshly ground black pepper

fresh basil leaves and flakes of Parmesan cheese, to serve

This is a lovely, rich-tasting mixture; I like to serve it with a simple green salad.

1 Fill a large saucepan with 4 litres / 7 pints of water and put it on the stove to heat up for the pasta.

2 Meanwhile, cook the leeks, either by sautéing in 1 tablespoon of oil or, for a less rich result, in a little boiling water. Either way they will take about 6 minutes. Drain the leeks if necessary and keep them warm.

3 When the water in the saucepan boils, add the pasta along with a tablespoon of salt and give the pasta a quick stir. Briefly put the lid on until it starts to lift, showing that the water has come back to the boil, then let the pasta bubble away, uncovered, for about 8 minutes, or until it is tender but still has some bite to it.

4 Meanwhile, heat the remaining oil in a saucepan and fry the mushrooms for 4–5 minutes until tender.

5 Drain the pasta by tipping it all into a colander placed in the sink, then put it back into the still-warm pan. Add the leeks, the mushrooms with their oil, sun-dried tomatoes and a seasoning of salt and pepper to taste. Serve the pasta onto warm plates, tear the basil over and scatter the Parmesan on top.

PENNE WITH ROASTED MEDITERRANEAN VEGETABLES Serves ❹

INGREDIENTS

1 aubergine, cut into 1cm / ½ inch dice

2 tablespoons olive oil

2 red peppers, de-seeded and cut into 1cm / ½ inch squares

2 yellow peppers, de-seeded and cut into 1cm / ½ inch squares

4 tomatoes, halved

4 large garlic cloves, peeled and chopped

salt and freshly ground black pepper

400g / 14oz penne

fresh basil leaves and flakes of Parmesan cheese, to serve

The vegetables for this recipe can be roasted ahead of time – the day before, even, if convenient, when the oven is on for something else. Then you can put the dish together very quickly, simply reheating the vegetables in the oven, grill or microwave before adding them to the cooked pasta.

1 Toss the aubergine in the olive oil, using your fingers to make sure that each piece is coated. Put the aubergine pieces into a shallow roasting tin with the peppers and roast in a medium-hot oven for 20 minutes. Then add the tomatoes and garlic and roast for a further 15–30 minutes, until all the vegetables are tender and lightly browned. Season with salt and pepper to taste.

2 Fill a large saucepan with 4 litres / 7 pints of water and put it on the stove to heat up for the pasta.

3 When the water boils, add the pasta along with a tablespoon of salt and give the pasta a quick stir. Briefly put the lid on until it starts to lift, showing that the water has come back to the boil, then let the pasta bubble away, uncovered, for about 8 minutes, or until it is tender but still has some bite to it.

4 Drain the pasta by tipping it all into a colander placed in the sink, then put it back into the still-warm pan and add the vegetables. Serve onto warm plates with torn basil and flakes of Parmesan on top.

SPAGHETTINI WITH TOFU, SOY SAUCE AND PEANUTS Serves ❹

INGREDIENTS

4 tablespoons soy sauce, such as Kikkoman

2 garlic cloves, peeled and crushed

1 teaspoon grated fresh ginger

1 dried red chilli, crumbled

300g / 10oz firm tofu, drained

400g / 14oz spaghettini

salt

groundnut or rapeseed oil

1 tablespoon sesame oil

4 spring onions, trimmed and chopped

2 – 4oz roasted peanuts, crushed

freshly ground black pepper

freshly chopped coriander leaves, to serve

This dish has an eastern flavour and a pleasant contrast of textures.

1 First prepare the tofu: this is best done at least half an hour before you start cooking the pasta, and can be done several hours in advance. Mix the soy sauce with the garlic, ginger and chilli. Cut the tofu into thin slices, spread these out in a single layer on a plate, then spoon the soy sauce mixture over, making sure all the tofu gets coated. Leave to marinate.

2 Fill a large saucepan with 4 litres / 7 pints of water and put it on the stove to heat up for the pasta.

3 When the water boils, add the spaghettini, holding it straight up like a bunch of flowers and gently pushing it into the water as it softens. Add a tablespoon of salt and give the pasta a quick stir. Briefly put the lid on until it starts to lift, showing that the water has come back to the boil, then let the pasta bubble away, uncovered, for about 8 minutes, or until it is tender but still has some bite to it.

4 Meanwhile, drain the tofu, reserving the marinade. Heat a little groundnut or rapeseed oil in a frying pan and fry the pieces of tofu for a minute or two on each side, until browned and crisp. Drain on kitchen paper and keep warm.

5 Drain the pasta by tipping it all into a colander placed in the sink, then put it back into the still-warm pan with the sesame oil, spring onions, peanuts, reserved marinade and black pepper to taste. Mix gently, then serve onto warm plates, topped with the tofu and generous amounts of coriander.

PIPE RIGATE WITH RED PEPPERS AND GARLIC Serves ❹

INGREDIENTS

4 red peppers

400g / 14oz pipe rigate

salt

2 fat juicy garlic cloves, peeled and thinly sliced

2 tablespoons olive oil

freshly ground black pepper

fresh basil leaves, to serve

As an alternative to grilling the peppers, you could roast them in the oven, as described on page 58. They can be done well ahead of time, when convenient, and reheated just before you want to use them.

1 Fill a large saucepan with 4 litres / 7 pints of water and put it on the stove to heat up for the pasta.

2 Next prepare the peppers by cutting them into quarters and placing, skin-side (shiny-side) up, on a grill pan. Put under a high heat for 10–15 minutes, until the skin has blistered and blackened in places. Cover the peppers with a plate and leave until cool enough to handle, then remove the skin, stem and seeds, and cut the flesh into strips.

3 When the water in the saucepan boils, add the pasta along with a tablespoon of

salt and give the pasta a quick stir. Briefly put the lid on until it starts to lift, showing that the water has come back to the boil, then let the pasta bubble away, uncovered, for about 8 minutes, or until it is tender but still has some bite to it.

4 Meanwhile, cook the garlic in the olive oil over a gentle heat for 2–3 minutes, without letting it brown. Keep on one side.

5 Drain the pasta by tipping it all into a colander placed in the sink, then put it back into the still-warm pan. Add the olive oil and garlic to the pasta, along with the pepper strips, toss gently, add salt and pepper to taste and serve onto warm plates, tearing basil over the top.

WHOLEWHEAT FUSILLI WITH GOAT'S CHEESE, SUN-DRIED TOMATOES AND BASIL Serves ❹

INGREDIENTS

400g / 14oz wholewheat fusilli

salt

1 tablespoon olive oil or oil from the sun-dried tomatoes

8 sun-dried tomatoes, chopped

225g / 8oz goat's cheese, diced or broken into small pieces

freshly torn basil leaves

freshly ground black pepper

The nutty flavour of wholewheat fusilli is a good foil for the intense flavour of the goat's cheese and sun-dried tomatoes.

1 Fill a large saucepan with 4 litres / 7 pints of water and put it on the stove to heat up for the pasta.

2 When the water boils, add the pasta along with a tablespoon of salt and give the pasta a quick stir. Briefly put the lid on until it starts to lift, showing that the water has come back to the boil, then let the pasta bubble away, uncovered, for about 8 minutes, or until it is tender but still has some bite to it.

3 Drain the pasta by tipping it all into a colander placed in the sink, then put it back into the still-warm pan, add the olive oil, sun-dried tomatoes, goat's cheese and basil, and salt and pepper to taste. Toss gently and serve onto warm plates.

FUSILLI WITH CHILLI, LEEKS AND COURGETTES Serves ❹

INGREDIENTS

olive oil

225g / 8oz leeks, trimmed and cut into 6mm / ¼ inch slices

1 fresh green chilli, de-seeded and chopped

225g / 8oz courgettes, trimmed and cut into matchsticks

400g / 14oz fusilli

salt and freshly ground black pepper

freshly grated pecorino cheese, to serve

This succulent mixture of pasta, leeks and courgettes is enlivened with chilli – add more or less, according to your taste.

1 Fill a large saucepan with 4 litres / 7 pints of water and put it on the stove to heat up for the pasta.

2 Meanwhile, heat 4 tablespoons of olive oil in a saucepan and put in the leeks and chilli. Cover and cook gently for 6–8 minutes, until the leeks are beginning to soften, then put in the courgettes and cook for a further 3–4 minutes, until the courgettes and leeks are tender. Keep the mixture warm.

3 When the water in the saucepan boils, add the pasta along with a tablespoon of salt and give the pasta a quick stir. Briefly put the lid on until it starts to lift, showing that the water has come back to the boil, then let the pasta bubble away, uncovered, for about 8 minutes, or until it is tender but still has some bite to it.

4 Drain the pasta by tipping it all into a colander placed in the sink, then put it back into the still-warm pan, add the leek mixture, season with salt and black pepper as necessary and toss gently. Serve onto warm plates, and hand round the pecorino.

PENNE RIGATE WITH TOMATOES, BASIL, PINE NUTS AND CHILLI Serves ❹

INGREDIENTS

2 tablespoons olive oil

900g / 2lb fresh tomatoes, skinned and chopped

2 fat juicy garlic cloves, peeled and thinly sliced

1 fresh green chilli, de-seeded and finely sliced

400g / 14oz penne rigate

salt

25–50g / 1–2oz pine nuts

4 good sprigs of fresh basil leaves, torn

freshly ground black pepper

I think of this as a summer dish – it is at its best when made with flavoursome, juicy plum tomatoes – but it can also bring some sunny warmth to a wintry day, made with whatever fresh tomatoes are available and a good kick of chilli.

1 Fill a large saucepan with 4 litres / 7 pints of water and put it on the stove to heat up for the pasta.

2 Meanwhile, heat the olive oil in a saucepan and put in the tomatoes, garlic and chilli. Cook gently, covered, for 10–15 minutes, until the tomatoes have collapsed.

3 When the water in the saucepan boils, add the pasta along with a tablespoon of salt and give the pasta a quick stir. Briefly put the lid on until it starts to lift, showing that the water has come back to the boil, then let the pasta bubble away, uncovered, for about 8 minutes, or until it is tender but still has some bite to it.

4 Drain the pasta by tipping it all into a colander placed in the sink, then put it back into the still-warm pan and add the tomato mixture, pine nuts and basil. Toss gently, season with salt and pepper, and serve onto warm plates.

NOODLES WITH MANGETOUT, WATER CHESTNUTS AND SWEETCORN Serves ❹

INGREDIENTS

2 tablespoons groundnut or rapeseed oil

2 garlic cloves, peeled and crushed

1 teaspoon grated fresh ginger

125g / 4oz mangetout, topped and tailed and sliced diagonally

125g / 4oz baby sweetcorn, sliced diagonally

125g / 4oz canned water chestnuts, drained and sliced

4 spring onions, trimmed and sliced diagonally

400g / 14oz noodles

2 tablespoons soy sauce, such as Kikkoman

salt and freshly ground black pepper

fresh coriander leaves, to serve

The delicious water chestnut is eaten fresh in Asia and available in cans here. Its crunchy texture contrasts well with the soft texture of the noodles. The noodles make this a very quick dish to prepare, since all they need is a brief soaking before being combined with the other ingredients. You could use other vegetables instead of the ones I have suggested – broccoli florets, red, yellow or green peppers or young green beans, for instance.

1 Heat the oil in a large saucepan and put in the garlic and ginger. Stir for 30 seconds, then add the mangetout, sweetcorn, water chestnuts and spring onions and stir-fry for 2–3 minutes, until the mixture is heated through.

2 Meanwhile, bring a kettleful of water to the boil. Put the noodles into a large bowl or saucepan, cover generously with boiling water and leave for 2–3 minutes (or according to the instructions on the packet) until tender, then drain them.

3 Add the noodles to the mangetout mixture in the pan, along with the soy sauce and salt and pepper as necessary, stir quickly over the heat and then serve immediately onto warm plates. Tear coriander leaves over the top.

FUSILLI LUNGHI WITH CHERRY TOMATOES, GREEN PEPPERS AND CAPERS Serves ❹

INGREDIENTS

2 tablespoons olive oil

2 green peppers, de-seeded and chopped

I fat juicy garlic clove, peeled and sliced

350g / 12oz cherry tomatoes, halved

400g / 14oz fusilli lunghi

salt

2 tablespoons capers

2 tablespoons freshly torn flat-leaf parsley

freshly ground black pepper

Pretty and piquant, this pasta dish makes the most of sweet cherry tomatoes. For an even more colourful effect, include some yellow cherry tomatoes in the mixture.

1 Fill a large saucepan with 4 litres / 7 pints of water and put it on the stove to heat up for the pasta.

2 Meanwhile, heat the oil in a saucepan, put in the peppers and garlic, cover and cook gently for about 15 minutes, until the peppers are tender, stirring from time to time. Then add the cherry tomatoes, cover and cook lightly for about 5 minutes.

3 When the water in the saucepan boils, add the pasta along with a tablespoon of salt and give the pasta a quick stir. Briefly put the lid on until it starts to lift, showing that the water has come back to the boil, then let the pasta bubble away, uncovered, for about 8 minutes, or until it is tender but still has some bite to it.

4 Drain the pasta by tipping it all into a colander placed in the sink, then put it back into the still-warm pan and add the green pepper and tomato mixture, the capers, the parsley, and salt and pepper to taste. Toss gently and serve onto warm plates.

PENNONI WITH CROÛTONS AND CARAMELIZED ONIONS Serves ❹

INGREDIENTS

olive oil

700g / 1½lb onions, preferably red, peeled and sliced

400g / 14oz pennoni

salt

4 slices of bread, crusts removed

freshly ground black pepper

freshly grated Parmesan cheese, to serve

This surprisingly good combination of textures and flavours can also be served with farfalle, or any other chunky pasta. The important thing is to cook the onions long enough, until meltingly tender and sweet.

1 First get the onions cooking. Heat 2 tablespoons of olive oil in a saucepan, put in the onions, stir, then cover and leave over a gentle heat for 30 minutes, until very tender. Stir from time to time, especially towards the end, to make sure they do not stick.

2 Fill a large saucepan with 4 litres / 7 pints of water and put it on the stove to heat up for the pasta.

3 When the water in the saucepan boils, add the pasta along with a tablespoon of salt and give the pasta a quick stir. Briefly put the lid on until it starts to lift, showing that the water has come back to the boil, then let the pasta bubble away, uncovered, for about 8 minutes, or until it is tender but still has some bite to it.

4 Meanwhile, make the croûtons. Fry the bread on both sides in a little hot olive oil, until crisp and golden. Cut into small squares and keep on one side.

5 Drain the pasta by tipping it all into a colander placed in the sink, then put it back into the still-warm pan and add the onions. Toss gently, season with salt and pepper and serve onto warm plates, scattering the croûtons on top. Parmesan goes well with this – hand it round separately.

RIGATONI WITH RED PEPPERS, SPINACH AND LENTILS Serves ❹

INGREDIENTS

2 large red peppers

400g / 14oz rigatoni

salt

225g / 8oz tender spinach, washed

2 tablespoons olive oil

100g / 3½oz brown or green lentils, cooked, or a 400g / 14oz can

squeeze of lemon juice

freshly ground black pepper

If you are using dry lentils, cook them first (no need to soak) in plenty of water until tender. This takes about 30 to 50 minutes, depending on the lentils, so keep checking them towards the end of their cooking time.

1 First prepare the peppers by cutting them into quarters and placing, skin-side (shiny-side) up, on a grill pan. Put under a high heat for 10–15 minutes, until the skin has blistered and blackened in places. Cover the peppers with a plate and leave until cool enough to handle, then remove the skin, stem and seeds, and cut the flesh into strips.

2 Fill a large saucepan with 4 litres / 7 pints of water and put it on the stove to heat up for the pasta.

3 When the water in the saucepan boils, add the pasta along with a tablespoon of salt and give the pasta a quick stir. Briefly put the lid on until it starts to lift, showing that the water has come back to the boil, then let the pasta bubble away, uncovered, for about 8 minutes, or until it is tender but still has some bite to it.

4 Meanwhile, dry the spinach on kitchen paper and cook in 1 tablespoon of the olive oil in a large saucepan for 2–3 minutes, or until it is just wilted. Add the lentils and their liquid and heat gently. Add a dash of lemon juice to taste and season with salt and pepper.

5 Drain the pasta by tipping it all into a colander placed in the sink, then put it back into the still-warm pan. Either add the remaining olive oil to the pasta, serve it onto warm plates and put the spinach mixture and the peppers on top; or add all of these directly to the pasta, toss gently and serve onto warm plates.

FUSILLI LUNGHI WITH BROCCOLI, GRILLED RED AND YELLOW PEPPER AND OLIVES Serves ❹

INGREDIENTS

1 large red pepper

1 large yellow pepper

400g / 14oz fusilli lunghi

salt

225g / 8oz prepared broccoli, cut into even-sized pieces

1 tablespoon olive oil

50g / 2oz black olives

freshly ground black pepper

fresh basil leaves and flakes of Parmesan cheese, to serve

Vibrant colours and intense flavours combine to make this an attractive dish. Grill the peppers well in advance, if you like, to save time later. If the peppers are to be served the same day, do not refrigerate them.

1 First prepare the peppers by cutting them into quarters and placing, skin-side (shiny-side) up, on a grill pan. Put under a high heat for 10–15 minutes, until the skin has blistered and blackened in places. Cover the pepper with a plate and leave until cool enough to handle, then remove the skin, stem and seeds, and cut the flesh into strips.

2 Fill a large saucepan with 4 litres / 7 pints of water and put it on the stove to heat up for the pasta.

3 When the water boils, add the pasta along with a tablespoon of salt and give the pasta a quick stir. Briefly put the lid on until it starts to lift, showing that the water has come back to the boil, then let the pasta bubble away, uncovered, for about 8 minutes, or until it is tender but still has some bite to it.

4 Meanwhile, cook the broccoli in a little boiling water for about 4 minutes, or until tender. Drain and keep warm.

5 Drain the pasta by tipping it all into a colander placed in the sink, then put it back into the still-warm pan with the olive oil, pepper strips, broccoli, olives and salt and pepper to taste. Stir gently, then serve the pasta onto warm plates. Tear the basil over and scatter the Parmesan on top.

RIGATONI WITH MUSHROOMS, LEEKS AND SUN-DRIED TOMATOES Serves ❹

INGREDIENTS

225g / 8oz leeks, trimmed and cut into 6mm / ¼ inch slices

olive oil

400g / 14oz rigatoni

salt

225g / 8oz mushrooms, washed and sliced

2 garlic cloves, peeled and crushed

8 sun-dried tomatoes, chopped

freshly ground black pepper

This is good just as it is, or it can be embellished with some chopped or torn parsley or basil and either Parmesan or pecorino cheese.

1 Fill a large saucepan with 4 litres / 7 pints of water and put it on the stove to heat up for the pasta.

2 Meanwhile, cook the leeks either in a little boiling water or in 2–3 tablespoons olive oil, with a lid on the pan, for 8–10 minutes until tender. Drain (if cooked in water) and keep warm.

3 When the water in the saucepan boils, add the pasta along with a tablespoon of salt and give the pasta a quick stir. Briefly put the lid on until it starts to lift, showing that the water has come back to the boil, then let the pasta bubble away, uncovered, for about 8 minutes, or until it is tender but still has some bite to it.

4 Fry the mushrooms in 2 tablespoons of olive oil, with the garlic, for 4–5 minutes, until tender and any liquid has boiled away. Mix together the leeks, mushrooms and sun-dried tomatoes, and season with salt and pepper.

5 Drain the pasta by tipping it all into a colander placed in the sink, then put it back into the still-warm pan. Either add a tablespoon of olive oil to the pasta, serve it onto plates and spoon the leek mixture on top; or add the leek mixture directly to the pasta, toss gently and serve onto warm plates.

LUMACHE WITH FETA CHEESE AND BROCCOLI Serves ❹

INGREDIENTS

400g / 14oz lumache

salt

450g / 1lb prepared broccoli, cut into 1cm / ½ inch pieces

1 tablespoon olive oil

125g / 4oz feta cheese

freshly ground black pepper

fresh basil leaves, to serve

There are lovely Mediterranean flavours in this simple pasta dish.

1 Fill a large saucepan with 4 litres / 7 pints of water and put it on the stove to heat up for the pasta.

2 When the water boils, add the pasta along with a tablespoon of salt and give the pasta a quick stir. Briefly put the lid on until it starts to lift, showing that the water has come back to the boil, then let the pasta bubble away, uncovered, for about 8 minutes, or until it is tender but still has some bite to it.

3 Meanwhile, cook the broccoli in a little boiling water for 3–4 minutes, or until it is just tender, then drain the broccoli and keep it warm.

4 Drain the pasta by tipping it all into a colander placed in the sink, then put it back into the still-warm pan with the olive oil, stirring gently so that the olive oil coats the pasta. Then add the feta and broccoli, check the seasoning, toss gently and serve onto warm plates. Tear the basil over the top.

PIPE RIGATE WITH AUBERGINE, RICOTTA AND BASIL Serves ❹

INGREDIENTS

2 aubergines, sliced then cut across into smaller pieces

salt

olive oil

2 fat juicy garlic cloves, peeled and sliced

freshly ground black pepper

400g / 14oz pipe rigate

225g / 8oz ricotta cheese

4 good sprigs of fresh basil leaves, torn

A wonderful contrast of different textures feature in this dish. Remember to allow an hour's salting time for the aubergines.

1 Put the aubergine pieces into a colander, sprinkle with salt and leave for an hour to draw out any bitter juices and also prevent the aubergine from absorbing too much oil when you fry it. Then rinse the aubergine under the tap and squeeze it dry.

2 Fill a large saucepan with 4 litres / 7 pints of water and put it on the stove to heat up for the pasta.

3 Heat 3 tablespoons of olive oil in a saucepan, put in the aubergine and the garlic, cover and leave to cook gently for about 20 minutes until the aubergine is tender. Stir the aubergine from time to time to prevent it from sticking. Season with salt and pepper.

4 When the water in the saucepan boils, add the pasta along with a tablespoon of salt and give the pasta a quick stir. Briefly put the lid on until it starts to lift, showing that the water has come back to the boil, then let the pasta bubble away, uncovered, for about 8 minutes, or until it is tender but still has some bite to it.

5 Drain the pasta by tipping it all into a colander placed in the sink, then put it back into the still-warm pan. Mix the ricotta in roughly with a fork, so that it is lumpy, then add the aubergine and basil. Toss gently, check the seasoning, and serve onto warm plates.

PENNONI WITH BROCCOLI, MASCARPONE, GARLIC AND FRESH BASIL Serves ❹

INGREDIENTS

400g / 14oz pennoni

salt

450g / 1lb prepared broccoli, cut into 1cm / ½ inch pieces

1 garlic clove, peeled and crushed

1 tablespoon olive oil

125g / 4oz mascarpone cheese

freshly ground black pepper

fresh basil leaves, to serve

The mascarpone cheese gives this recipe a delectable creaminess but could be replaced with a low-fat smooth white cheese.

1 Fill a large saucepan with 4 litres / 7 pints of water and put it on the stove to heat up for the pasta.

2 When the water boils, add the pasta along with a tablespoon of salt and give the pasta a quick stir. Briefly put the lid on until it starts to lift, showing that the water has come back to the boil, then let the pasta bubble away, uncovered, for about 8 minutes, or until it is tender but still has some bite to it.

3 Meanwhile, cook the broccoli in a little boiling water for 3–4 minutes, or until just tender, then drain and keep warm.

4 Cook the garlic in the olive oil over a gentle heat for 2–3 minutes, without letting it brown. Keep on one side.

5 Drain the pasta by tipping it all into a colander placed in the sink, then put it back into the still-warm pan with the garlic, along with its oil, stirring gently so that the oil coats the pasta. Add the mascarpone cheese and broccoli, check the seasoning and serve onto warm plates. Tear the basil over the top.

FARFALLE WITH CARROTS, GOAT'S CHEESE, THYME AND SUN-DRIED TOMATOES Serves ❹

INGREDIENTS

400g / 14oz farfalle

salt

2 large carrots, scraped

8 sun-dried tomatoes, chopped

4 good sprigs of thyme, leaves crumbled

1 tablespoon olive oil or oil from the sun-dried tomatoes

225g / 8oz goat's cheese, diced or broken into small pieces

freshly ground black pepper

An unusual combination of ingredients which works really well – try it! You can use either a soft white goat's cheese log or the kind with a rind.

1 Fill a large saucepan with 4 litres / 7 pints of water and put it on the stove to heat up for the pasta.

2 When the water boils, add the pasta along with a tablespoon of salt and give the pasta a quick stir. Briefly put the lid on until it starts to lift, showing that the water has come back to the boil, then let the pasta bubble away, uncovered, for about 8 minutes, or until it is tender but still has some bite to it.

3 Meanwhile, heat another, smaller pan with water for the carrots. Grate the carrots, then blanch them for 1 minute in the pan of water. Drain and return to the pan with the sun-dried tomatoes and thyme. Keep warm.

4 Drain the pasta by tipping it all into a colander placed in the sink, then put it back into the still-warm pan, add the olive or sun-dried tomato oil, carrot mixture and goat's cheese, with salt and pepper to taste. Toss gently and serve onto warm plates.

PENNE WITH RED ONIONS, GOAT'S CHEESE AND WALNUTS Serves ❹

INGREDIENTS

2 tablespoons olive oil

700g / 1½lb red onions, peeled and thinly sliced

400g / 14oz penne

salt

125g / 4oz smooth goat's cheese, roughly chopped

50g / 2oz shelled walnuts, preferably freshly cracked

freshly ground black pepper

A nice autumn mixture, making the most of new season walnuts and the strong flavours of red onions and goat's cheese. If you do not like goat's cheese, you could use any smooth white creamy cheese instead.

1 First get the onions cooking. Heat the olive oil in a saucepan, put in the onions, stir, then cover and leave over a gentle heat for 30 minutes, until very tender. Stir from time to time, especially towards the end, to make sure they do not stick.

2 Fill a large saucepan with 4 litres / 7 pints of water and put it on the stove to heat up for the pasta.

3 When the water boils, add the pasta along with a tablespoon of salt and give the pasta a quick stir. Briefly put the lid on until it starts to lift, showing that the water has come back to the boil, then let the pasta bubble away, uncovered, for about 8 minutes, or until it is tender but still has some bite to it.

4 Drain the pasta by tipping it all into a colander placed in the sink, then put it back into the still-warm pan, add the goat's cheese and toss gently. Then add the onions and walnuts, and salt and pepper to taste, and serve onto warm plates.

PIPE RIGATE WITH SWISS CHARD, MASCARPONE AND PINE NUTS Serves ❹

INGREDIENTS

450g / 1lb Swiss chard, washed

2 tablespoons olive oil

salt and freshly ground black pepper

400g / 14oz pipe rigate

125g / 4oz mascarpone cheese

50g / 2oz pine nuts, toasted (see page 78)

Swiss chard is delicious if you can get it; if not, use tender spinach instead, cooking it for just 2–3 minutes until wilted.

1 Fill a large saucepan with 4 litres / 7 pints of water and put it on the stove to heat up for the pasta.

2 Separate the leafy part of the Swiss chard from the stems. Cut the stems into 1cm / ½ inch lengths, then gently cook in the olive oil for about 7 minutes until just tender. Add the leafy parts and cook for a further 4 minutes or until these are tender, too. Season with salt and pepper.

3 When the water boils, add the pasta along with a tablespoon of salt and give the pasta a quick stir. Briefly put the lid on until it starts to lift, showing that the water has come back to the boil, then let the pasta bubble away, uncovered, for about 8 minutes, or until it is tender but still has some bite to it.

4 Drain the pasta by tipping it all into a colander placed in the sink, then put it back into the still-warm pan, add the Swiss chard, mascarpone and pine nuts, toss gently and serve onto warm plates.

VERMICELLI WITH CHICKPEAS Serves ❹

INGREDIENTS

2 x 400g / 14oz cans chickpeas

400g / 14oz vermicelli

salt

2–4 tablespoons olive oil

2 garlic cloves, peeled and crushed

freshly ground black pepper

1–2 tablespoons chopped fresh parsley, to serve, optional

2 tablespoons sesame seeds, toasted (see page 78), to serve

This is a classic Italian dish known as *tuono e lampo* – 'thunder and lightning', which refers to the contrasting textures of the pasta and chickpeas.

1 Put the chickpeas, together with their liquid, into a saucepan and heat gently.

2 Fill a large saucepan with 4 litres / 7 pints of water and put it on the stove to heat up for the pasta.

3 When the water boils, add the pasta along with a tablespoon of salt and give the pasta a quick stir. Briefly put the lid on until it starts to lift, showing that the water has come

back to the boil, then cook the vermicelli, uncovered, for 3–4 minutes, or until it is tender but still has some bite to it, stirring all the time so that the thin strands do not stick together.

4 Drain the pasta by tipping it all into a colander placed in the sink, then put it back into the still-warm pan with 2–4 tablespoons of olive oil, to your taste, the garlic and a few grindings of pepper.

5 Add the chickpeas to the pasta, toss gently and serve onto warmed plates. Sprinkle with the parsley, if using, and the sesame seeds.

VEGETABLE CHOW MEIN Serves ❹

INGREDIENTS

2 tablespoons roasted sesame oil

8 spring onions, trimmed and sliced

1 garlic clove, peeled and crushed

1 red pepper, de-seeded and chopped

125g / 4oz baby sweetcorn, cut into 1cm / ½ inch lengths

125g / 4oz mushrooms, washed and sliced

1 tablespoon cornflour

2 tablespoons soy sauce

2 tablespoons sherry

150ml / 5fl oz vegetable stock

400g / 14oz vermicelli

salt

1 tablespoon olive oil

1–2 tablespoons sesame seeds

This is good as a main course on its own or as part of a Chinese meal along with some stir-fried vegetables and boiled rice. Hand round soy sauce at the table for people to add more if they wish.

1 Fill a large saucepan with 4 litres / 7 pints of water and put it on the stove to heat up for the pasta.

2 Meanwhile, heat the sesame oil in a large saucepan and put in the spring onions, garlic, red pepper, sweetcorn and mushrooms. Fry for 5 minutes, stirring often.

3 Put the cornflour into a small bowl or cup and add the soy sauce, sherry and stock. Pour this mixture into the saucepan with the vegetable mixture, bring to the boil and cook for 1 minute, stirring. Remove from the heat and set aside while you cook the pasta.

4 When the water in the saucepan boils, add the pasta along with a tablespoon of salt and give the pasta a quick stir. Briefly put the lid on until it starts to lift, showing that the water has come back to the boil, then cook the vermicelli, uncovered, for 3–4 minutes, or until it is tender but still has some bite to it, stirring all the time so that the thin strands do not stick together.

5 Drain the pasta by tipping it all into a colander placed in the sink, then put it back into the still-warm pan with the olive oil. Stir gently and leave on one side.

6 Quickly reheat the vegetable mixture, then pour it in with the pasta. Toss gently, serve onto warmed plates and sprinkle with the sesame seeds.

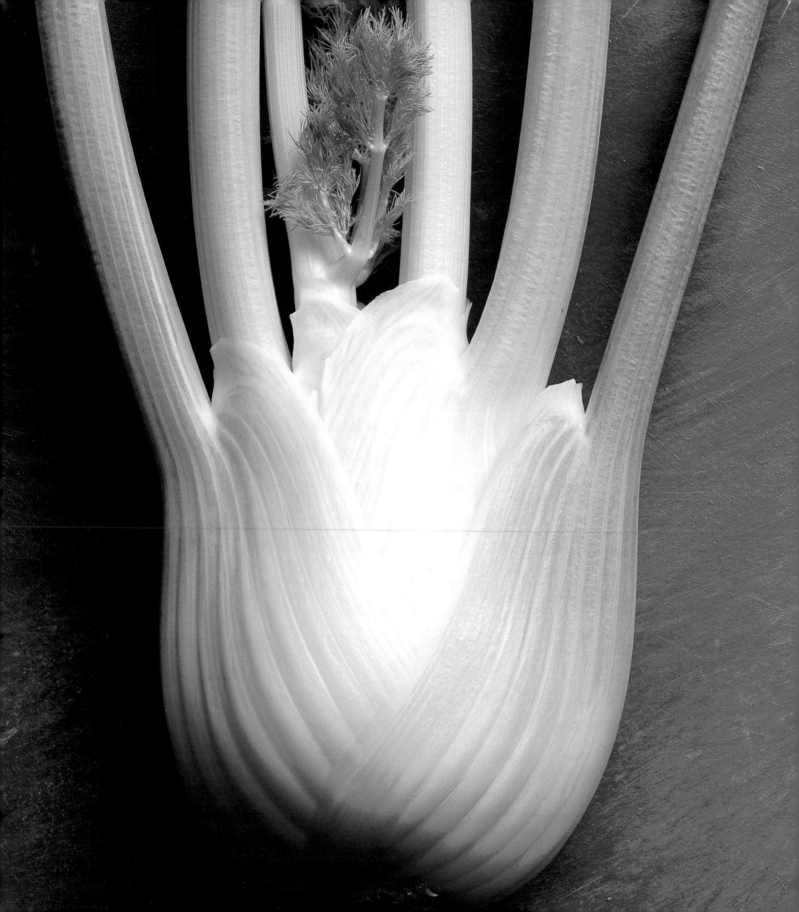

The Classic Sauces

Here you will find five classic sauces, each followed by recipes which add other ingredients to create a variety of different dishes. Once you have made the basic sauce, you have many possibilities before you. Three of the basic sauces – tomato, béchamel and lentil bolognese – freeze very well, so it can be helpful to make a double quantity and put one lot away in the freezer for another day. The pesto and cream sauces keep well, tightly covered, in the refrigerator: pesto for up to two weeks, cream sauce for a couple of days.

While pesto, cream sauce, béchamel and tomato sauce are all indisputably 'classic', you might think I am stretching things a bit when I include in this section lentil bolognese sauce. I have included it because while it may not be a classic sauce in the sense that the others are, it is definitely a classic as far as vegetarian cookery is concerned, and a most useful and nutritious sauce as well. If you want something filling to keep the chill out on a winter's night, then this is the one for you.

Béchamel sauce fell into disrepute for a time in foodie circles a few years ago, perhaps because it was over-used in recipes where a lighter touch would have been preferable. However, it is certainly a classic sauce, and delicious if well made. Like other recipes in this book which contain milk or cream, béchamel sauce can be very satisfactorily made with soya milk and cream and, indeed, these are what I prefer to use instead of dairy milk.

PESTO Serves ❹

INGREDIENTS

50g / 2oz fresh basil leaves

2 garlic cloves, peeled

2 tablespoons pine nuts, toasted

8 tablespoons olive oil

50g / 2oz freshly grated Parmesan cheese, optional

salt and freshly ground black pepper

squeeze of lemon juice, optional

• VARIATION •
SLIMMER'S PESTO

Replace 4 tablespoons of the oil with virtually fat-free fromage frais, or, to reduce calories further, with water.

Recipes for classic pesto sauce vary slightly and some people argue details but, quite honestly, when a recipe contains basil, garlic, olive oil, pine nuts and Parmesan you really cannot go wrong! It is also a basic idea that can be successfully adapted in a number of ways, as the following recipes show.

1 Put the basil leaves, garlic cloves and pine nuts into a food processor or blender, with a little of the olive oil if necessary for the machine to work, and whizz to a fairly smooth paste. (A blender needs a little liquid in order to work, while a food processor can often start off with 'dry' ingredients.)

2 Gradually add the rest of the oil, whizzing as you go, then transfer the mixture to a bowl, or to a screw-top jar if you are planning to keep the pesto in the fridge. Stir in the Parmesan cheese, if using.

3 Season with salt and pepper and add a squeeze of lemon juice to bring out the flavour if you think it needs it. Either use immediately, adding the pesto directly to hot, cooked spaghetti, tagliatelle or other pasta, or keep it in the fridge for up to 2 weeks.

•

A jar of pesto keeps well in the fridge. Besides being wonderful on pasta it is great on bread: spread it on slices of bread and grill or bake. You can also top baked potatoes with pesto, and add it to a simple béchamel sauce as well as to vegetable and pasta soups and pasta bakes.

You can make pesto in the traditional way using a pestle and mortar if you like. It takes longer, but the method is the same, with elbow power replacing the action of a machine.

For how to toast pine nuts, see page 78.

PENNE WITH CHILLI PESTO Serves ❹

INGREDIENTS

400g / 14oz penne

salt

FOR THE PESTO:

50g / 2oz fresh basil leaves

2 garlic cloves, peeled

2 tablespoons pine nuts, toasted

1–2 fresh green chillies, de-seeded

8 tablespoons olive oil

salt and freshly ground black pepper

squeeze of lemon juice, optional

Fresh chilli gives a kick to this pesto: add it judiciously, according to the type of chillies you are using and to your taste. You may prefer to chop the chilli finely and stir it in at the end, bit by bit, until you get your desired degree of heat.

1 Fill a large saucepan with 4 litres / 7 pints of water and put it on the stove to heat up for the pasta.

2 Meanwhile, make the pesto – or this can be done well in advance if you prefer. Follow the recipe given above, pulverizing the chillies along with the basil and the other ingredients and leaving out the Parmesan cheese.

3 When the water in the saucepan boils, add the pasta along with a tablespoon of salt and give the pasta a quick stir. Briefly put the lid on until it starts to lift, showing that the water has come back to the boil, then let the pasta bubble away, uncovered, for about 8 minutes, or until it is tender but still has some bite to it.

4 Scoop up half a mugful of water from the pasta and set aside. Drain the pasta into a colander placed in the sink, then put it back into the still-warm pan. Loosen the pesto, if it needs it, by mixing in a couple of tablespoons of the hot pasta water, then add it to the pasta. Toss the pasta gently until well coated with the pesto, check the seasoning, then serve at once onto warm plates.

SPAGHETTI WITH CORIANDER AND CHILLI PESTO WITH RED PEPPER Serves ❹

INGREDIENTS

400g / 14oz spaghetti

salt

½ red pepper, de-seeded and finely chopped, to serve

FOR THE PESTO:

50g / 2oz fresh coriander leaves

2 garlic cloves, peeled

1 dried red chilli, crumbled

2 tablespoons pine nuts, toasted

8 tablespoons olive oil

salt and freshly ground black pepper

squeeze of lemon juice, optional

Coriander makes a pesto with a difference and the flecks of red chilli look pretty and add their own punch – you may not need much, depending on your taste.

1 Fill a large saucepan with 4 litres / 7 pints of water and put it on the stove to heat up for the pasta.

2 Meanwhile, make the pesto – or this can be done well in advance if you prefer. Follow the recipe opposite, using coriander instead of basil, adding the chilli with the garlic and leaving out the Parmesan cheese.

3 When the water in the saucepan boils, add the spaghetti, holding it straight up like a bunch of flowers and gently pushing it into the water as it softens. Add a tablespoon of salt and give the pasta a quick stir. Briefly put the lid on until it starts to lift, showing that the water has come back to the boil, then let the pasta bubble away, uncovered, for about 8 minutes, or until it is tender but still has some bite to it.

4 Scoop up about half a mugful of water from the pasta and set aside. Drain the pasta by tipping it all into a colander placed in the sink, then put it back into the still-warm pan. Loosen the pesto, if it needs it, by mixing in a couple of tablespoons of the hot pasta water, then add it to the pasta. Toss the pasta gently until well coated, check the seasoning, then serve at once onto warm plates, and sprinkle with the chopped red pepper.

PENNE WITH SUN-DRIED TOMATO PESTO, FRESH BASIL AND PARMESAN Serves ❹

INGREDIENTS

400g / 14oz penne

salt

fresh basil leaves and flakes of Parmesan cheese, to serve

FOR THE PESTO:

50g / 2oz sun-dried tomatoes

2 garlic cloves, peeled

2 tablespoons pine nuts, toasted

8 tablespoons oil – from the tomatoes plus olive oil to make up

salt and freshly ground black pepper

squeeze of lemon juice, optional

A lovely sunny mixture of flavours in this unconventional pesto. Use sun-dried tomatoes in oil and drain before weighing.

1 Fill a large saucepan with 4 litres / 7 pints of water and put it on the stove to heat up for the pasta.

2 Meanwhile, make the pesto – or this can be done well in advance if you prefer. Follow the recipe opposite, using sun-dried tomatoes instead of basil.

3 When the water in the saucepan boils, add the pasta along with a tablespoon of salt and give the pasta a quick stir. Briefly put the lid on until it starts to lift, showing that the water has come back to the boil, then let the pasta bubble away, uncovered, for about 8 minutes, or until it is tender but still has some bite to it.

4 Scoop up about half a mugful of water from the pasta and set aside. Drain the pasta by tipping it all into a colander placed in the sink, then put it back into the still-warm pan. Loosen the pesto, if it needs it, by mixing in a couple of tablespoons of the hot pasta water, then add it to the pasta. Toss the pasta gently until well coated, check the seasoning, then serve at once onto warm plates, tearing basil leaves over the top and scattering with Parmesan.

SPAGHETTI WITH CHILLI—RED-PEPPER PESTO Serves ❹

INGREDIENTS

400g / 14oz spaghetti

salt

fresh basil leaves, to serve, optional

FOR THE PESTO:

1 red pepper

2 garlic cloves, peeled

2 tablespoons pine nuts, toasted

1 dried red chilli, optional

8 tablespoons olive oil

salt and freshly ground black pepper

squeeze of lemon juice, optional

Scarlet and warming, chilli—red-pepper pesto goes well with most of the more substantial pastas, and with tagliatelle and penne too.

1 First prepare the pepper for the pesto by cutting it into quarters and placing, skin-side (shiny-side) up, on a grill pan. Put under a high heat for 10–15 minutes, until the skin has blistered and blackened in places. Cover the pepper with a plate and leave until cool enough to handle, then remove the skin, stem and seeds, and cut the flesh into slices.

2 Fill a large saucepan with 4 litres / 7 pints of water and put it on the stove to heat up for the pasta.

3 Meanwhile, make the pesto – or this can be done well in advance if you prefer. Follow the recipe on page 76, using the red pepper instead of the basil, adding the red chilli, if using, and leaving out the Parmesan.

4 When the water in the saucepan boils, add the spaghetti, holding it straight up like a bunch of flowers and gently pushing it into the water as it softens. Add a tablespoon of salt and give the pasta a quick stir. Briefly put the lid on until it starts to lift, showing that the water has come back to the boil, then let the pasta bubble away, uncovered, for about 8 minutes, or until it is tender but still has some bite to it.

5 Scoop up about half a mugful of water from the pasta and set aside. Drain the pasta by tipping it all into a colander placed in the sink, then put it back into the still-warm pan. Give the pesto a stir and loosen it a bit, if it needs it, by mixing in a couple of tablespoons of the hot pasta water, then add it to the pasta. Toss the pasta gently until it is all coated with the pesto, check the seasoning, then serve at once onto warm plates. Tear some basil over the top if you like.

•

To toast pine nuts, spread them out in a single layer in a grill pan and put under a hot grill until they turn golden brown and smell toasted. This will happen very quickly, in a minute or two, so do not take your eyes off them. Give them a stir halfway through so that both sides get toasted evenly. Other nuts, such as walnuts, pecans or flaked almonds, can be toasted in the same way. So too can sesame seeds, but they take only seconds.

SPAGHETTI WITH OLIVE PESTO Serves ❹

INGREDIENTS

400g / 14oz spaghetti

salt

fresh basil or flat-leaf parsley,
to serve

FOR THE PESTO:

50g / 2oz pitted black olives

2 garlic cloves, peeled

2 tablespoons pine nuts, toasted
(see page 78)

1 dried red chilli, optional

8 tablespoons olive oil

salt and freshly ground black pepper

squeeze of lemon juice, optional

This is a rich-tasting pesto in which the flavour of the olives really comes out. A mixed salad of lettuce, tomato and basil goes well with it, and some warm bread.

1 Fill a large saucepan with 4 litres / 7 pints of water and put it on the stove to heat up for the pasta.

2 Meanwhile, make the pesto – or this can be done well in advance if you prefer. Follow the recipe on page 76, using the olives instead of the basil, adding the chilli, if using, with the other ingredients and leaving out the Parmesan.

3 When the water in the saucepan boils, add the spaghetti, holding it straight up like a bunch of flowers and gently pushing it into the water as it softens. Add a tablespoon of salt and give the pasta a quick stir. Briefly put the lid on until it starts to lift, showing that the water has come back to the boil, then let the pasta bubble away, uncovered, for about 8 minutes, or until it is tender but still has some bite to it.

4 Scoop up about half a mugful of water from the pasta and set aside. Drain the pasta by tipping it all into a colander placed in the sink, then put it back into the still-warm pan. Give the pesto a stir and loosen it a bit, if it needs it, by mixing in a couple of tablespoons of the hot pasta water, then add it to the pasta. Toss the pasta gently until it is all coated with the pesto, check the seasoning, then serve at once onto warm plates. Tear or snip basil or flat-leaf parsley over the top.

CONCHIGLIE WITH PARSLEY PESTO AND ARTICHOKE HEARTS Serves ❹

INGREDIENTS

400g / 14oz conchiglie

salt

a 400g / 14oz can artichoke
hearts, drained and sliced

FOR THE PESTO:

50g / 2oz fresh parsley leaves

2 garlic cloves, peeled

2 tablespoons pine nuts, toasted
(see page 78)

8 tablespoons olive oil

50g / 2oz freshly grated Parmesan

salt and freshly ground black pepper

squeeze of lemon juice, optional

Curly or flat-leaf parsley will do for this pesto. I use canned artichoke hearts, because I like them and they do not have any added fat, but use a jar of artichokes in oil if you prefer.

1 Fill a large saucepan with 4 litres / 7 pints of water and put it on the stove to heat up for the pasta.

2 Meanwhile, make the pesto – or this can be done well in advance if you prefer. Follow the recipe on page 76, using parsley instead of basil.

3 When the water in the saucepan boils, add the pasta along with a tablespoon of salt and give the pasta a quick stir. Briefly put the lid on until it starts to lift, showing that the water has come back to the boil, then let the pasta bubble away, uncovered, for about 8 minutes, or until it is tender but still has some bite to it.

4 Scoop up about half a mugful of water from the pasta and set aside. Drain the pasta by tipping it all into a colander placed in the sink, then put it back into the still-warm pan. Give the pesto a stir and loosen it a bit, if it needs it, by mixing in a couple of tablespoons of the hot pasta water, then add it to the pasta. Toss the pasta gently until it is all coated with the pesto, then add the artichoke hearts. Check the seasoning, and serve at once onto warm plates.

FETTUCCINE WITH MINT PESTO AND PEAS Serves ❹

INGREDIENTS

400g / 14oz fettuccine

salt

225g / 8oz podded fresh peas or frozen petits pois

FOR THE PESTO:

50g / 2oz fresh mint leaves

2 garlic cloves, peeled

2 tablespoons pine nuts, toasted (see page 78)

8 tablespoons olive oil

salt and freshly ground black pepper

squeeze of lemon juice, optional

A lovely, refreshing, summery pesto, perfect with a delicate egg pasta such as fettuccine. Fresh peas are best, otherwise use tender young frozen peas – petits pois.

1 Fill a large saucepan with 4 litres / 7 pints of water and put it on the stove to heat up for the pasta.

2 Meanwhile, make the pesto – or this can be done well in advance if you prefer. Follow the recipe on page 76, using mint instead of basil and leaving out the Parmesan cheese.

3 When the water in the saucepan boils, add the pasta along with a tablespoon of salt and give the pasta a quick stir. Briefly put the lid on until it starts to lift, showing that the water has come back to the boil, then let the pasta bubble away, uncovered, for about 8 minutes, or until it is tender but still has some bite to it.

4 While the fettuccine is cooking, bring 1cm / ½ inch of water to the boil for the peas. Cook them for 2–3 minutes, then drain.

5 Scoop up about half a mugful of water from the pasta and set aside. Drain the pasta by tipping it all into a colander placed in the sink, then put it back into the still-warm pan. Give the pesto a stir and loosen it a bit, if it needs it, by mixing in a couple of tablespoons of the hot pasta water, then add it to the pasta, along with the peas. Toss the pasta gently until it is all coated with the pesto, check the seasoning, then serve at once onto warm plates.

FUSILLI LUNGHI WITH CRUNCHY NUT PESTO Serves ❹

INGREDIENTS

400g / 14oz fusilli lunghi

salt

fresh parsley, preferably flat-leaf, to serve

FOR THE PESTO:

50g / 2oz walnuts, pecans or cashew nuts, toasted

2 tablespoons pine nuts, toasted (see page 78)

2 garlic cloves, peeled

1 tablespoon soy sauce

4 tablespoons olive oil

salt and freshly ground black pepper

squeeze of lemon juice, optional

Pesto made with extra nuts is crunchy, delicious, and best, I think, with a fairly substantial pasta.

1 Fill a large saucepan with 4 litres / 7 pints of water and put it on the stove to heat up for the pasta.

2 Meanwhile, make the pesto – or this can be done well in advance if you prefer. Follow the recipe on page 76, leaving out the Parmesan and using the nuts instead of the basil, only 4 tablespoons of oil, a tablespoon of soy sauce and 3 tablespoons of water.

3 When the water in the saucepan boils, add the pasta along with a tablespoon of salt and give the pasta a quick stir. Briefly put the lid on until it starts to lift, showing that the water has come back to the boil, then let the pasta bubble away, uncovered, for about 8 minutes, or until it is tender but still has some bite to it.

4 Scoop up about half a mugful of water from the pasta and set aside. Drain the pasta by tipping it all into a colander placed in the sink, then put it back into the still-warm pan. Give the pesto a stir and loosen it a bit, if it needs it, by mixing in a couple of tablespoons of the hot pasta water, then add it to the pasta. Toss the pasta gently until it is all coated with the pesto, check the seasoning, then serve at once onto warm plates. Tear or snip the parsley over the top.

CREAM SAUCE Serves ❹

INGREDIENTS

25g / 1oz butter

1 onion, peeled and chopped

2 garlic cloves, peeled and crushed

300ml / 10fl oz cream — single, double or soya cream

salt and freshly ground black pepper

freshly grated nutmeg

This rich sauce is wonderful for a special meal. It can be made with double cream for the most classic and, of course, luscious result, but both single dairy cream and the single soya creams now available also give very good results.

1 Melt the butter in a small saucepan, then add the onion. Cover and cook gently for 10 minutes, until tender but not brown.

2 Add garlic to the onion and cook for a minute or two longer. Stir in the cream and leave the mixture to simmer gently for about 10 minutes, until the cream has reduced a bit and thickened.

3 Season with salt, pepper and nutmeg and keep on one side until the pasta is done.

TAGLIATELLE WITH GORGONZOLA CREAM SAUCE Serves ❹

INGREDIENTS

400g / 14oz tagliatelle

salt

1 quantity of cream sauce (above)

125g / 4oz Gorgonzola cheese, diced

1 tablespoon olive oil, optional

freshly ground black pepper

This is rich and wonderful. You could use another type of blue cheese if you prefer, and, as for the cream sauce, the single-cream version is best since the cheese adds so much richness.

1 Fill a large saucepan with 4 litres / 7 pints of water and put it on the stove to heat up for the pasta.

2 When the water boils, add the pasta along with a tablespoon of salt and give the pasta a quick stir. Briefly put the lid on until it starts to lift, showing that the water has come back to the boil, then let the pasta bubble away, uncovered, for about 8 minutes, or until it is tender but still has some bite to it.

3 Heat the cream sauce through gently. Just before the pasta is ready, remove the sauce from the heat and add the Gorgonzola, so that it begins to melt.

4 Drain the pasta by tipping it all into a colander placed in the sink, then put it back into the still-warm pan. Either add the olive oil to the pasta, serve it onto warm plates and spoon the sauce on top; or add the sauce directly to the pasta, toss gently and serve onto warm plates. Grind some black pepper coarsely over the top and serve at once.

FUSILLI IN CREAM SAUCE WITH ASPARAGUS AND SUMMER HERBS Serves ❹

INGREDIENTS

450g / 1lb asparagus, trimmed and cut into 2.5cm / 1 inch lengths

400g / 14oz fusilli

salt

1 quantity of cream sauce (opposite)

freshly ground black pepper

squeeze of lemon juice, optional

1 tablespoon olive oil

2 tablespoons chopped or torn fresh flat-leaf parsley, chervil and chives, to serve

A wonderful summer pasta dish; serve it with a delicate, leafy salad and chilled white wine.

1 Fill a large saucepan with 4 litres / 7 pints of water and put it on the stove to heat up for the pasta.

2 Meanwhile, cook the asparagus in a little boiling water for 6–8 minutes, or until tender. Drain the asparagus and keep it warm.

3 When the water in the saucepan boils, add the pasta along with a tablespoon of salt and give the pasta a quick stir. Briefly put the lid on until it starts to lift, showing that the water has come back to the boil, then let the pasta bubble away, uncovered, for about 8 minutes, or until it is tender but still has some bite to it.

4 Heat the cream sauce through gently. Add the asparagus and check the seasoning, adding pepper, a squeeze of lemon juice and salt to taste if it needs it.

5 Drain the pasta by tipping it all into a colander placed in the sink, then put it back into the still-warm pan. Either add the olive oil to the pasta, serve it onto warm plates and spoon the sauce on top; or add the sauce directly to the pasta, toss gently and serve onto warm plates. Scatter the herbs on top and serve at once.

PAPPARDELLE IN CREAM SAUCE WITH PORCINI Serves ❹

INGREDIENTS

400g / 14oz pappardelle

salt

25g / 1oz butter

350g /12oz fresh porcini
mushrooms, washed and sliced

1 garlic clove, peeled and crushed

1 quantity of cream sauce (page 82)

squeeze of lemon juice, optional

freshly ground black pepper

1 tablespoon olive oil, optional

sprigs of fresh flat-leaf parsley,
to serve

If you are lucky enough to be able to get some, fresh porcini (also called ceps) are a wonderful treat. If porcini are unavailable, or the price too ridiculous, use oyster or fresh shiitake mushrooms instead.

1 Fill a large saucepan with 4 litres / 7 pints of water and put it on the stove to heat up for the pasta.

2 When the water boils, add the pasta along with a tablespoon of salt and give the pasta a quick stir. Briefly put the lid on until it starts to lift, showing that the water has come back to the boil, then let the pasta bubble away, uncovered, for about 8 minutes, or until it is tender but still has some bite to it.

3 Meanwhile, cook the porcini mushrooms. Melt the butter in a medium saucepan, add the mushrooms and garlic and cook for 4–5 minutes, or until the mushrooms are tender and any liquid has disappeared, stirring from time to time. Keep the porcini mushrooms warm.

4 Heat the cream sauce through gently. Check the seasoning, adding a squeeze of lemon juice if it needs it.

5 Drain the pasta by tipping it all into a colander placed in the sink, then put it back into the still-warm pan. Either add the olive oil to the pasta, serve it onto warm plates and spoon the sauce on top; or add the sauce directly to the pasta, toss gently and serve onto warm plates. Spoon the porcini on top, tear or snip the parsley over, and serve at once.

TAGLIATELLE IN CREAM SAUCE WITH GRUYÈRE, PARMESAN AND FLAT-LEAF PARSLEY Serves ❹

INGREDIENTS

400g / 14oz tagliatelle

salt

1 quantity of cream sauce (page 82)

100g / 3½oz Gruyère
cheese, grated

50g / 2oz freshly grated
Parmesan cheese

1 tablespoon olive oil, optional

freshly ground black pepper

sprigs of fresh parsley, preferably
flat-leaf, to serve

As this is rich with added cheeses, I find the single-cream version of the cream sauce is best. It is for when you feel like a soothing, indulgent dish.

1 Fill a large saucepan with 4 litres / 7 pints of water and put it on the stove to heat up for the pasta.

2 When the water boils, add the pasta along with a tablespoon of salt and give the pasta a quick stir. Briefly put the lid on until it starts to lift, showing that the water has come back to the boil, then let the pasta bubble away, uncovered, for about 8 minutes, or until it is tender but still has some bite to it.

3 Heat the cream sauce through gently. Just before the pasta is done, add all the Gruyère and half of the Parmesan cheese to the sauce.

4 Drain the pasta by tipping it all into a colander placed in the sink, then put it back into the still-warm pan. Either add the olive oil to the pasta, serve it onto warm plates and spoon the sauce on top; or add the sauce directly to the pasta, toss gently and serve onto warm plates. Coarsely grind some black pepper to taste over the pasta, scatter with the remaining Parmesan cheese and tear the sprigs of parsley over the top. Serve at once.

FETTUCCINE IN CREAM SAUCE WITH FRESH PEAS AND MINT Serves ❹

INGREDIENTS

400g / 14oz fettuccine

salt

450g / 1lb podded tender fresh peas or frozen petits pois

1 quantity of cream sauce (page 82)

freshly ground black pepper

1 tablespoon olive oil, optional

2–3 tablespoons chopped fresh mint leaves, to serve

This is wonderful with tender fresh peas, but also very good with frozen petits pois.

1 Fill a large saucepan with 4 litres / 7 pints of water and put it on the stove to heat up for the pasta.

2 When the water boils, add the pasta along with a tablespoon of salt and give the pasta a quick stir. Briefly put the lid on until it starts to lift, showing that the water has come back to the boil, then let the pasta bubble away, uncovered, for about 8 minutes, or until it is tender but still has some bite to it.

3 Add the peas to the cream sauce in a pan and cook over a gentle heat, to heat through both the peas and the sauce. Check the seasoning, adding a little salt and pepper to taste if it needs it.

4 Drain the pasta by tipping it all into a colander placed in the sink, then put it back into the still-warm pan. Either add the olive oil to the pasta, serve it onto warm plates and spoon the sauce on top; or add the sauce directly to the pasta, toss gently and serve onto warm plates. Scatter the chopped mint on top and serve at once.

FETTUCCINE WITH DOLCELATTE CREAM SAUCE AND SPINACH Serves ❹

INGREDIENTS

400g / 14oz fettuccine

salt

1 quantity of cream sauce (page 82)

125g / 4oz dolcelatte cheese, cut into small cubes

125g / 4oz tender spinach leaves, finely shredded

freshly ground black pepper

1 tablespoon olive oil, optional

If you cannot get dolcelatte, use any other type of blue cheese for this delicious dish.

1 Fill a large saucepan with 4 litres / 7 pints of water and put it on the stove to heat up for the pasta.

2 When the water boils, add the pasta along with a tablespoon of salt and give the pasta a quick stir. Briefly put the lid on until it starts to lift, showing that the water has come back to the boil, then let the pasta bubble away, uncovered, for about 8 minutes, or until it is tender but still has some bite to it.

3 Heat the cream sauce through gently. Just before the pasta is ready, add the dolcelatte and spinach to the sauce and stir for 1–2 minutes over the heat. Season with some pepper – it probably will not need any salt because the cheese will have added some.

4 Drain the pasta by tipping it all into a colander placed in the sink, then put it back into the still-warm pan. Either add the olive oil to the pasta, serve it onto warm plates and spoon the sauce on top; or add the sauce directly to the pasta, toss gently and serve onto warm plates.

TAGLIATELLE VERDE IN CREAM SAUCE WITH OYSTER MUSHROOMS AND GARLIC Serves ❹

INGREDIENTS

400g / 14oz tagliatelle verde

salt

25g / 1oz butter

350g / 12oz oyster mushrooms, washed and sliced

1 garlic clove, peeled and crushed

1 quantity of cream sauce (page 82)

freshly ground black pepper

squeeze of lemon juice, optional

1 tablespoon olive oil

sprigs of fresh flat-leaf parsley, to serve

Oyster mushrooms, with their delicate flavour and texture, are excellent in this dish.

1 Fill a large saucepan with 4 litres / 7 pints of water and put it on the stove to heat up for the pasta.

2 When the water boils, add the pasta along with a tablespoon of salt and give the pasta a quick stir. Briefly put the lid on until it starts to lift, showing that the water has come back to the boil, then let the pasta bubble away, uncovered, for about 8 minutes, or until it is tender but still has some bite to it.

3 Meanwhile, cook the oyster mushrooms: melt the butter in a medium saucepan, add the mushrooms and garlic and cook for 4–5 minutes, or until the mushrooms are tender and any liquid has disappeared, stirring from time to time.

4 Heat the cream sauce through gently. Add the mushrooms and check the seasoning, adding pepper, a squeeze of lemon juice and salt to taste if it needs it.

5 Drain the pasta by tipping it all into a colander placed in the sink, then put it back into the still-warm pan. Either add the olive oil to the pasta, serve it onto warm plates and spoon the sauce on top; or add the sauce directly to the pasta, toss gently and serve onto warm plates. Chop, snip or tear the parsley over the top.

PENNE WITH CHILLI-CREAM SAUCE Serves ❹

INGREDIENTS

400g / 14oz penne

salt

1 dried red chilli, crumbled

1 tablespoon sun-dried tomato purée

1 quantity of cream sauce (page 82)

freshly ground black pepper

1 tablespoon olive oil, optional

fresh basil leaves, to serve

The chilli takes the richness away from the sauce and gives it an unexpected and pleasant note.

1 Fill a large saucepan with 4 litres / 7 pints of water and put it on the stove to heat up for the pasta.

2 When the water boils, add the pasta along with a tablespoon of salt and give the pasta a quick stir. Briefly put the lid on until it starts to lift, showing that the water has come back to the boil, then let the pasta bubble away, uncovered, for about 8 minutes, or until it is tender but still has some bite to it.

3 Stir the chilli and sun-dried tomato purée into the cream sauce in a pan and heat through gently. Check the seasoning, adding salt and pepper to taste if it needs it.

4 Drain the pasta by tipping it all into a colander placed in the sink, then put it back into the still-warm pan. Either add the olive oil to the pasta, serve it onto warm plates and spoon the sauce on top; or add the sauce directly to the pasta, toss gently and serve onto warm plates. Tear the basil leaves over the top and serve at once.

FUSILLI IN CREAM SAUCE WITH YOUNG SUMMER VEGETABLES Serves ❹

INGREDIENTS

125g / 4oz baby new carrots, trimmed and scrubbed

225g / 8oz asparagus, trimmed and cut into 1cm / ½ inch lengths

400g / 14oz fusilli

salt

225g / 8oz podded fresh broad beans

1 quantity of cream sauce (page 82)

125g / 4oz podded fresh peas

freshly ground black pepper

squeeze of lemon juice, optional

1 tablespoon olive oil, optional

sprigs of fresh chervil, to serve

Another summery dish, although you could make it at any time of the year when you feel like a taste of sunshine.

1 Fill a large saucepan with 4 litres / 7 pints of water and put it on the stove to heat up for the pasta.

2 Meanwhile, cook the baby carrots and asparagus in a little boiling water for 6–8 minutes, or until they are tender; drain the vegetables and keep them warm.

3 When the water in the saucepan boils, add the pasta along with a tablespoon of salt and give the pasta a quick stir. Briefly put the lid on until it starts to lift, showing that the water has come back to the boil, then let the pasta bubble away, uncovered, for about 8 minutes, or until it is tender but still has some bite to it.

4 Meanwhile, blanch the broad beans in boiling water for 1 minute; drain, refresh under the cold tap then pop the beans out of their skins.

5 Add the broad beans to the cream sauce in a pan, along with the peas, and heat through gently. Just before the pasta is ready, add the carrots and asparagus to the cream sauce. Check the seasoning, adding a few grindings of pepper and a squeeze of lemon juice to taste if it needs it.

6 Drain the pasta by tipping it all into a colander placed in the sink, then put it back into the still-warm pan. Either add the olive oil to the pasta, serve it onto warm plates and spoon the sauce on top; or add the sauce directly to the pasta, toss gently and serve onto warm plates. Scatter some sprigs of chervil on top and serve at once.

BÉCHAMEL SAUCE Serves ❹

INGREDIENTS

50g / 2oz butter

40g / 1½oz flour

600ml / 1 pint milk

1 bay leaf

a few stalks of parsley if available

slice of onion if available

a little extra milk — see method

60–120ml / 4–8 tablespoons cream, optional

salt and freshly ground black pepper

freshly grated nutmeg

Classic béchamel sauce is comforting and makes a good base for variations. If you want to reduce the calories, use skimmed milk (or soya milk) and omit the cream, or try the completely non-classic but useful slimmer's béchamel sauce which follows.

1 Melt the butter in a saucepan and stir in the flour. When it froths, stir in half the milk and beat well over the heat until it thickens. Add the rest of the milk and keep stirring vigorously, still over the heat, until the sauce is thick and smooth.

2 Add the bay leaf, parsley stalks and slice of onion if using, then leave the sauce over a very low heat for 10 minutes. Thin the sauce by stirring in a little extra milk if necessary. If you are making the sauce well in advance, do not stir in this extra milk but pour it over the top of the sauce and leave it, to prevent a skin forming.

3 When you are ready to use the sauce, give it a stir, remove the bay leaf, parsley and onion, add the cream if using and season with salt, pepper and nutmeg.

•

Whizz béchamel in a blender if it is lumpy – this also seems to make the sauce taste creamier, so I often do it anyway.

SLIMMER'S BÉCHAMEL SAUCE Serves ❹

INGREDIENTS

25g / 1oz cornflour

600ml / 1 pint semi-skimmed milk or unsweetened soya milk

1 bay leaf

a few stalks of parsley if available

slice of onion if available

1 tablespoon Dijon mustard

salt and freshly ground black pepper

freshly grated nutmeg

a little extra milk, optional — see method

This is a very useful sauce for anyone who is watching their calories. It is surprisingly flavoursome and makes an excellent base for adding other interesting ingredients. You can substitute this for ordinary béchamel in any of the recipes.

1 Put the cornflour into a bowl and mix to a thin paste with a little of the milk. Bring the rest of the milk to the boil with the bay leaf, and the parsley and slice of onion if using.

2 Pour the boiling milk over the cornflour mixture, stirring well, then tip the whole lot back into the pan. Stir over a moderate heat for a couple of minutes until the mixture has thickened, then remove from the heat. Stir in the mustard and season with salt, pepper and nutmeg.

3 If you are making the sauce well in advance, pour a little milk over the surface of the sauce and leave it to prevent a skin forming.

4 When you are ready to use the sauce, remove the bay leaf, onion and parsley. Give the sauce a stir and check the seasoning, adding salt, pepper and nutmeg to taste if it needs it.

LUMACHE WITH BROCCOLI BÉCHAMEL Serves ❹

Broccoli and béchamel is a winning combination. I like to serve this pasta dish with a tomato salad – perhaps little cherry tomatoes, halved and tossed in a light vinaigrette – and some warm bread for those who want it. Other short pastas could be used: gnocchi or conchiglie, for instance.

1 Fill a large saucepan with 4 litres / 7 pints of water and put it on the stove to heat up for the pasta.

2 When the water boils, add the pasta along with a tablespoon of salt and give the pasta a quick stir. Briefly put the lid on until it starts to lift, showing that the water has come back to the boil, then let the pasta bubble away, uncovered, for about 8 minutes, or until it is tender but still has some bite to it.

3 Meanwhile, cook the broccoli in a little boiling water for 3–4 minutes, or until it is just tender, then drain and add to the béchamel sauce.

4 Heat the béchamel sauce through gently and check the seasoning, adding pepper, nutmeg, a squeeze of lemon juice and more salt to taste if it needs it.

5 Drain the pasta by tipping it all into a colander placed in the sink, then put it back into the still-warm pan. Either add the olive oil to the pasta, serve it onto warm plates and spoon the sauce on top; or add the sauce directly to the pasta, toss gently and serve onto warm plates.

SPAGHETTI WITH BÉCHAMEL SAUCE, PESTO AND PARMESAN Serves ❹

You could use homemade pesto (page 76) for this, or one of the good bottled ones which are now available.

1 Fill a large saucepan with 4 litres / 7 pints of water and put it on the stove to heat up for the pasta.

2 When the water boils, add the spaghetti, holding it straight up like a bunch of flowers and gently pushing it into the water as it softens. Add a tablespoon of salt and give the pasta a quick stir. Briefly put the lid on until it starts to lift, showing that the water has come back to the boil, then let the pasta bubble away, uncovered, for about 8 minutes, or until it is tender but still has some bite to it.

3 Meanwhile, heat the béchamel sauce through gently. Stir in the pesto and check the seasoning, adding salt and pepper as necessary.

4 Drain the spaghetti by tipping it all into a colander placed in the sink, then put it back into the still-warm pan. Either add the olive oil to the pasta, serve it onto warm plates and spoon the sauce on top; or add the sauce directly to the pasta, toss gently and serve onto warm plates. Scatter generously with the Parmesan and tear or snip the parsley or basil over the top.

TAGLIATELLE IN MUSHROOM AND GARLIC BÉCHAMEL SAUCE WITH PARSLEY Serves ❹

INGREDIENTS

400g / 14oz tagliatelle

salt

25g / 1oz butter

450g / 1lb mushrooms, washed and sliced

2 garlic cloves, peeled and crushed

1 quantity of béchamel sauce or slimmer's béchamel sauce (page 90)

freshly ground black pepper

squeeze of lemon juice, optional

1 tablespoon olive oil, optional

bunch of fresh flat-leaf parsley

freshly grated Parmesan cheese, to serve

This is good made with tagliatelle, but the short pastas are also suitable, particularly a chunky one such as gnocchi or lumache.

1 Fill a large saucepan with 4 litres / 7 pints of water and put it on the stove to heat up for the pasta.

2 When the water boils, add the pasta along with a tablespoon of salt and give the pasta a quick stir. Briefly put the lid on until it starts to lift, showing that the water has come back to the boil, then let the pasta bubble away, uncovered, for about 8 minutes, or until it is tender but still has some bite to it.

3 Meanwhile, cook the mushrooms: melt the butter in a medium saucepan, add the mushrooms and garlic and cook for 4–5 minutes, or until tender and any liquid has disappeared, stirring from time to time.

4 Heat the béchamel sauce through gently, stir in the mushrooms and check the seasoning, adding pepper, a squeeze of lemon juice and salt to taste if it needs it.

5 Drain the tagliatelle by tipping it all into a colander placed in the sink, then put it back into the still-warm pan. Either add the olive oil to the pasta, serve it onto warm plates and spoon the sauce on top; or add the sauce directly to the pasta, toss gently and serve onto warm plates. Tear or snip plenty of parsley over the top, and hand round freshly grated Parmesan.

CONCHIGLIE WITH BÉCHAMEL SAUCE, FRESH HERBS AND PINE NUTS Serves ❹

INGREDIENTS

400g / 14oz conchiglie

salt

1 quantity of béchamel sauce or slimmer's béchamel sauce (page 90)

5–6 tablespoons chopped fresh herbs: parsley, chives, and chervil if available

freshly ground black pepper

squeeze of lemon juice, optional

50g / 2oz pine nuts, toasted (see page 78)

1 tablespoon olive oil, optional

sprigs of fresh parsley and flakes of Parmesan cheese, to serve

This is simple but very good: the fresh herbs really make it, and the pine nuts give a pleasant crunch, as well as adding flavour.

1 Fill a large saucepan with 4 litres / 7 pints of water and put it on the stove to heat up for the pasta.

2 When the water boils, add the pasta along with a tablespoon of salt and give the pasta a quick stir. Briefly put the lid on until it starts to lift, showing that the water has come back to the boil, then let the pasta bubble away, uncovered, for about 8 minutes, or until it is tender but still has some bite to it.

3 Meanwhile, heat the béchamel sauce through gently, then stir in the herbs and check the seasoning, adding some grindings of pepper and a squeeze of lemon juice to taste if it needs it.

4 Drain the pasta by tipping it all into a colander placed in the sink, then put it back into the still-warm pan. Add the pine nuts to the pan. Either add the olive oil to the pasta, serve it onto warm plates and spoon the sauce on top; or add the sauce directly to the pasta, toss gently and serve onto warm plates. Decorate with sprigs of parsley and scatter the flakes of Parmesan over the top.

FUSILLI AND SWEETCORN IN BÉCHAMEL SAUCE WITH RED AND GREEN PEPPERS Serves ❹

INGREDIENTS

400g / 14oz fusilli

salt

225g / 8oz fresh sweetcorn scraped from the cob or frozen or canned sweetcorn

1 quantity of béchamel sauce or slimmer's béchamel sauce (page 90)

1 small red pepper, de-seeded and finely chopped

1 small green pepper, de-seeded and finely chopped

freshly ground black pepper

squeeze of lemon juice, optional

1 tablespoon olive oil, optional

I have found this dish to be popular with children, all of whom seem to like sweetcorn and enjoy the bright colours of the peppers. Use their favourite pasta shape: butterflies (farfalle), shells (conchiglie) or snails (lumache) are as good as spirals (fusilli).

1 Fill a large saucepan with 4 litres / 7 pints of water and put it on the stove to heat up for the pasta.

2 When the water boils, add the pasta along with a tablespoon of salt and give the pasta a quick stir. Briefly put the lid on until it starts to lift, showing that the water has come back to the boil, then let the pasta bubble away, uncovered, for about 8 minutes, or until it is tender but still has some bite to it.

3 Meanwhile, cook the sweetcorn in a little boiling water for 3–4 minutes, or until it is just tender, then drain and add to the béchamel sauce along with the chopped peppers.

4 Heat the béchamel sauce through gently, then check the seasoning, adding pepper, a squeeze of lemon juice and salt to taste if it needs it.

5 Drain the pasta by tipping it all into a colander placed in the sink, then put it back into the still-warm pan. Either add the olive oil to the pasta, serve it onto warm plates and spoon the sauce on top; or add the sauce directly to the pasta, toss gently and serve onto warm plates.

SPINACH TAGLIATELLE WITH BÉCHAMEL SAUCE AND THREE CHEESES Serves ❹

INGREDIENTS

400g / 14oz spinach tagliatelle (tagliatelle verde)

salt

2 x 125g / 4oz firm goat's cheese log, each sliced into 4 rounds

1 quantity of béchamel sauce or slimmer's béchamel sauce (page 90)

50g / 2oz freshly grated Parmesan cheese

freshly ground black pepper

1 tablespoon olive oil

125g / 4oz blue cheese, crumbled

sprigs of flat-leaf parsley, to serve

You could use a different selection of cheeses than those given here, but choose three contrasting ones so that the flavours are distinct because they soften and melt in the hot sauce.

1 Fill a large saucepan with 4 litres / 7 pints of water and put it on the stove to heat up for the pasta.

2 When the water boils, add the pasta along with a tablespoon of salt and give the pasta a quick stir. Briefly put the lid on until it starts to lift, showing that the water has come back to the boil, then let the pasta bubble away, uncovered, for about 8 minutes, or until it is tender but still has some bite to it.

3 Just before the pasta is done, set the grill to high. Line the grill pan with foil and place the rounds of goat's cheese on it; grill for 3–4 minutes until they are golden brown and beginning to melt.

4 Heat the béchamel sauce through gently. Stir in half the Parmesan cheese and check the seasoning, adding salt and pepper as necessary.

5 Drain the pasta by tipping it all into a colander placed in the sink, then put it back into the still-warm pan. Add the olive oil and toss gently. Serve the pasta onto warmed plates, spoon the sauce on top then scatter with the blue cheese and remaining Parmesan and place two circles of goat's cheese on each serving. Garnish with a few sprigs of flat-leaf parsley.

FARFALLE WITH BÉCHAMEL SAUCE, GRILLED FENNEL AND PINE NUTS Serves ❹

INGREDIENTS

450g / 1lb fennel bulbs, trimmed, reserving any feathery leaves, and sliced into eighths

olive oil

400g / 14oz farfalle

salt

1 quantity of béchamel sauce or slimmer's béchamel sauce (page 90)

freshly ground black pepper

squeeze of lemon juice, optional

50g / 2oz pine nuts, toasted (see page 78)

Grilled fennel is easy to do and a delicious ingredient in this pasta dish. If you do not like fennel, or cannot get it, use grilled pepper strips instead. The dish would be rather different, but also very good.

1 Fill a large saucepan with 4 litres / 7 pints of water and put it on the stove to heat up for the pasta.

2 Meanwhile, par-boil the fennel in a little boiling water for 4–5 minutes until just tender. Then drain well, brush lightly all over with olive oil, put in a single layer on a grill pan or baking sheet that will fit under your grill, and grill under a high heat until tender and tinged with brown: 4–5 minutes. Keep the fennel warm.

3 When the water in the saucepan boils, add the pasta along with a tablespoon of salt and give the pasta a quick stir. Briefly put the lid on until it starts to lift, showing that the water has come back to the boil, then let the pasta bubble away, uncovered, for about 8 minutes, or until it is tender but still has some bite to it.

4 Heat the béchamel sauce through gently. Chop any reserved fennel leaves and add to the sauce. Check the seasoning, adding a squeeze of lemon juice if it needs it.

5 Drain the pasta by tipping it all into a colander placed in the sink, then put it back into the still-warm pan. Either add 1 tablespoon of olive oil to the pasta, serve it onto warm plates and spoon the sauce on top; or add the sauce directly to the pasta, toss gently and serve onto warm plates. In either case, top with slices of grilled fennel and toasted pine nuts and serve at once.

FARFALLE BÉCHAMEL WITH LEEKS, OLIVES, AND SUN-DRIED TOMATOES Serves ❹

INGREDIENTS

450g / 1lb leeks, trimmed and cut into 6mm / ¼ inch slices

8 sun-dried tomatoes, drained of oil and roughly chopped

125g / 4oz black olives

400g / 14oz farfalle

salt

1 quantity of béchamel sauce or slimmer's béchamel sauce (page 90)

freshly ground black pepper

squeeze of lemon juice, optional

1 tablespoon olive oil, optional

fresh flat-leaf parsley and flakes of Parmesan cheese, to serve

This is a wonderfully tasty, filling mixture. It doesn't need any accompaniment except perhaps some warm bread – a wholewheat walnut loaf – if you are very hungry.

1 Fill a large saucepan with 4 litres / 7 pints of water and put it on the stove to heat up for the pasta.

2 Meanwhile, cook the leeks in a little boiling water for about 6 minutes, until tender. Drain the leeks, return them to the pan and add the sun-dried tomatoes and olives.

3 When the water in the saucepan boils, add the pasta along with a tablespoon of salt and give the pasta a quick stir. Briefly put the lid on until it starts to lift, showing that the water has come back to the boil, then let the pasta bubble away, uncovered, for about 8 minutes, or until it is tender but still has some bite to it.

4 Heat the béchamel sauce through gently and add half the leek mixture. Check the seasoning, adding a squeeze of lemon juice if it needs it.

5 Drain the pasta by tipping it all into a colander placed in the sink, then put it back into the still-warm pan. Either add the olive oil to the pasta, serve it onto warm plates and spoon the sauce on top; or add the sauce directly to the pasta, toss gently and serve onto warm plates. Top with the remaining leek mixture, tear or snip a little parsley over, scatter with the Parmesan and serve at once.

FETTUCCINE BÉCHAMEL WITH GRILLED ASPARAGUS, LEMON AND PARSLEY Serves ❹

INGREDIENTS

400g / 14oz fettuccine

salt

450g / 1lb asparagus, trimmed and halved to make pieces approx. 5cm / 2 inches long

olive oil

1 quantity of béchamel sauce or slimmer's béchamel sauce (page 90)

freshly ground black pepper

squeeze of lemon juice, optional

finely shredded rind of 1 lemon

flakes of Parmesan cheese, to serve

Grilling is a very good way to cook asparagus; it is easier than boiling or steaming it, and the result is excellent. If you want to save a few calories, though, better boil or steam it.

1 Fill a large saucepan with 4 litres / 7 pints of water and put it on the stove to heat up for the pasta.

2 When the water boils, add the pasta along with a tablespoon of salt and give the pasta a quick stir. Briefly put the lid on until it starts to lift, showing that the water has come back to the boil, then let the pasta bubble away, uncovered, for about 8 minutes, or until it is tender but still has some bite to it.

3 Meanwhile, brush the asparagus with a little olive oil and grill under a high heat until tender and lightly browned: 6–8 minutes, turning the asparagus over half way through.

4 Heat the béchamel sauce through gently. Check the seasoning, adding pepper and a squeeze of lemon juice to taste if it needs it.

5 Drain the pasta by tipping it all into a colander placed in the sink, then put it back into the still-warm pan. Either add 1 tablespoon of olive oil to the pasta, serve it onto warm plates and spoon the sauce on top; or add the sauce directly to the pasta, toss gently and serve onto warm plates. Top with the asparagus and lemon zest (rind). Scatter with Parmesan, grind black pepper over and serve at once.

•

A citrus zester is quite cheap to buy and very useful. Grasp the lemon, or other citrus fruit, and run the zester firmly down its skin to produce long slim ribbons of zest with no pith attached. If you do not have a zester, pare off thin slices of skin with a potato peeler then cut into thin shreds.

LENTIL BOLOGNESE SAUCE Serves ❹

INGREDIENTS

125g / 4oz whole green or brown lentils or split orange lentils, or a 400g / 14oz can of green lentils

1 onion, peeled and chopped

2 tablespoons olive oil

2 garlic cloves, peeled and crushed

1 celery stick, chopped

1 carrot, finely diced

2 tomatoes, skinned and chopped

1 teaspoon sun-dried tomato purée

1 tablespoon chopped parsley

salt and freshly ground black pepper

Lentils – indeed, any pulses – make a great combination with pasta: protein-packed and filling. A lentil sauce makes a good vegetarian version of a bolognese sauce and lots of variations are possible. You can use either whole lentils or the split orange ones – each gives a different result, and both are good.

1 If you are using any type of dried lentils, put them into a saucepan with 500ml / 18fl oz of water and bring to the boil, then let them simmer gently until they are tender: 40 minutes or so for the brown or green lentils, about 20 minutes for the orange ones. Drain the lentils, whether freshly cooked or canned, keeping the liquid.

2 Fry the onion in the oil for 5 minutes, then add the garlic, celery and carrots. Cover and leave to cook gently for 15 minutes until tender, stirring from time to time.

3 Add the lentils, tomatoes, sun-dried tomato purée and enough of the reserved liquid to make a thick, soft consistency. Simmer for about 10 minutes, adding more liquid if necessary. Stir in the parsley and season with salt and freshly ground black pepper.

SPAGHETTI WITH LENTIL BOLOGNESE SAUCE AND SUN-DRIED TOMATOES Serves ❹

INGREDIENTS

400g / 14oz spaghetti

salt

8 sun-dried tomatoes, drained of oil and roughly chopped

1 quantity of lentil bolognese sauce (above)

freshly ground black pepper

1 tablespoon olive oil, optional

sprigs of fresh parsley or chervil, to serve

fresh Parmesan cheese, cut in flakes or grated, to serve

The sun-dried tomatoes add a lovely richness to this sauce. It is good with both spaghetti and tagliatelle.

1 Fill a large saucepan with 4 litres / 7 pints of water and put it on the stove to heat up for the pasta.

2 When the water boils, add the spaghetti, holding it straight up like a bunch of flowers and gently pushing it into the water as it softens. Add a tablespoon of salt and give the pasta a quick stir. Briefly put the lid on until it starts to lift, showing that the water has come back to the boil, then let the pasta bubble away, uncovered, for about 8 minutes, or until it is tender but still has some bite to it.

3 Meanwhile, stir the chopped sun-dried tomatoes into the bolognese sauce in a pan and heat through gently. Check the seasoning, adding salt and pepper to taste if it needs it.

4 Drain the pasta by tipping it all into a colander placed in the sink, then put it back into the still-warm pan. Either add the olive oil to the pasta, serve it onto warm plates and spoon the sauce on top; or add the sauce directly to the pasta, toss gently and serve onto warm plates. Tear the parsley or chervil over the top, scatter with Parmesan flakes and serve at once.

TAGLIATELLE WITH LENTIL AND WINE SAUCE Serves ❹

INGREDIENTS

400g / 14oz tagliatelle

salt

glass of red wine

1 quantity of lentil bolognese sauce (opposite)

freshly ground black pepper

1 tablespoon olive oil, optional

fresh basil leaves and flakes of Parmesan cheese, to serve

This is rich-tasting and warming; great to come back to on a chilly winter's night.

1 Fill a large saucepan with 4 litres / 7 pints of water and put it on the stove to heat up for the pasta.

2 When the water boils, add the pasta along with a tablespoon of salt and give the pasta a quick stir. Briefly put the lid on until it starts to lift, showing that the water has come back to the boil, then let the pasta bubble away, uncovered, for about 8 minutes, or until it is tender but still has some bite to it.

3 Meanwhile, add the wine to the bolognese sauce in a pan, bring to the boil then let simmer gently. Check the seasoning, adding salt and pepper to taste if it needs it.

4 Drain the pasta by tipping it all into a colander placed in the sink, then put it back into the still-warm pan. Either add the olive oil to the pasta, serve it onto warm plates and spoon the sauce on top; or add the sauce directly to the pasta, toss gently and serve onto warm plates. Tear basil leaves over the top, scatter with flakes of Parmesan and serve at once.

FUSILLI LUNGHI WITH MUSHROOMS IN LENTIL BOLOGNESE SAUCE Serves ❹

INGREDIENTS

400g / 14oz fusilli lunghi

salt

225g / 8oz mushrooms, washed and sliced

olive oil

2 garlic cloves, peeled and crushed

1 quantity of lentil bolognese sauce (opposite)

freshly ground black pepper

fresh Parmesan cheese, cut in flakes or grated, to serve

1 Fill a large saucepan with 4 litres / 7 pints of water and put it on the stove to heat up for the pasta.

2 When the water boils, add the pasta along with a tablespoon of salt and give the pasta a quick stir. Briefly put the lid on until it starts to lift, showing that the water has come back to the boil, then let the pasta bubble away, uncovered, for about 8 minutes, or until it is tender but still has some bite to it.

3 Fry the mushrooms in 1 tablespoon of olive oil, with the garlic, for 4–5 minutes, until tender and any liquid has boiled away.

4 Add the mushrooms to the bolognese sauce in a pan and heat through gently. Check the seasoning, adding salt and pepper to taste if it needs it.

5 Drain the pasta by tipping it all into a colander placed in the sink, then put it back into the still-warm pan. Either add 1 tablespoon of olive oil to the pasta, serve it onto warm plates and spoon the sauce on top; or add the sauce directly to the pasta, toss gently and serve onto warm plates. Serve at once and hand around the Parmesan.

PENNE RIGATE WITH GOLDEN LENTIL BOLOGNESE SAUCE, RED PEPPER AND LEEKS Serves ❹

INGREDIENTS

2 red peppers

225g / 8oz leeks, trimmed and cut into 6mm / ¼ inch slices

olive oil, optional

400g / 14oz penne rigate

salt

1 quantity of lentil bolognese sauce (page 100), made with split orange lentils

freshly ground black pepper

A flavoursome combination of ingredients, this colourful pasta dish is filling and needs no accompaniment, except perhaps a glass of red wine.

1 First prepare the peppers for the sauce by cutting them into quarters and placing them, skin-side (shiny-side) up, on a grill pan. Put under a high heat for 10–15 minutes, until the skin has blistered and blackened in places. Cover the peppers with a plate and leave until cool enough to handle, then remove the skin, stem and seeds, and cut the flesh into slices.

2 Fill a large saucepan with 4 litres / 7 pints of water and put it on the stove to heat up for the pasta.

3 Meanwhile, cook the leeks, either by sautéing them in 1 tablespoon of olive oil or, for a less rich result, in a little boiling water. Either way they will take about 6 minutes. Drain the leeks if necessary and keep them warm.

4 When the water in the saucepan boils, add the pasta along with a tablespoon of salt and give the pasta a quick stir. Briefly put the lid on until it starts to lift, showing that the water has come back to the boil, then let the pasta bubble away, uncovered, for about 8 minutes, or until it is tender but still has some bite to it.

5 Heat the bolognese sauce through gently. Check the seasoning, adding salt and pepper to taste if it needs it.

6 Drain the pasta by tipping it all into a colander placed in the sink, then put it back into the still-warm pan. Either add the olive oil to the pasta, serve it onto warm plates and spoon the sauce on top; or add the sauce directly to the pasta, toss gently and serve onto warm plates. Put the peppers and leeks on top and serve at once.

SPAGHETTI WITH LENTIL BOLOGNESE, FRESH PEAS AND MINT Serves ❹

INGREDIENTS

400g / 14oz spaghetti

salt

1 quantity of lentil bolognese sauce (page 100)

225g / 8oz podded fresh peas or frozen petit pois

freshly ground black pepper

1 tablespoon olive oil, optional

2–3 tablespoons chopped fresh mint

The peas and mint give a surprisingly light, summery feeling to this hearty pasta dish. A tomato salad goes well with it.

1 Fill a large saucepan with 4 litres / 7 pints of water and put it on the stove to heat up for the pasta.

2 When the water boils, add the spaghetti, holding it straight up like a bunch of flowers and gently pushing it into the water as it softens. Add a tablespoon of salt and give the pasta a quick stir. Briefly put the lid on until it starts to lift, showing that the water has come back to the boil, then let the pasta bubble away, uncovered, for about 8 minutes, or until it is tender but still has some bite to it.

3 Meanwhile, gently reheat the bolognese sauce. Just before the pasta is done, add the peas to the sauce and cook gently for a minute or two, to heat the peas through. Check the seasoning, adding salt and pepper to taste if it needs it.

4 Drain the pasta by tipping it all into a colander placed in the sink, then put it back into the still-warm pan. Either add the olive oil to the pasta, serve it onto warm plates and spoon the sauce on top; or add the sauce directly to the pasta, toss gently and serve on to warm plates. Scatter the mint on top and serve at once.

LASAGNETTE WITH SPICED LENTIL AND TOMATO BOLOGNESE SAUCE Serves ❹

INGREDIENTS

½ a 400g / 14oz can tomatoes

½ teaspoon ground cinnamon

1 teaspoon chopped fresh oregano or ½ teaspoon dried oregano

1 quantity of lentil bolognese sauce (page 100), made with split orange lentils

salt and freshly ground black pepper

400g / 14oz lasagnette

1 tablespoon olive oil, optional

sprigs of fresh oregano and freshly grated Parmesan cheese, to serve

Here, extra tomatoes, cinnamon and oregano are added to the basic sauce – and I think the sauce works better in this case made with split orange lentils rather than whole lentils.

1 Fill a large saucepan with 4 litres / 7 pints of water and put it on the stove to heat up for the pasta.

2 Meanwhile, add the tomatoes, cinnamon and oregano to the bolognese sauce in a pan, breaking up the tomatoes with the spoon as you do so. Cook over a fairly gentle heat for 10–15 minutes, until the tomatoes have reduced. Check the seasoning, adding salt and pepper to taste if it needs it.

3 When the water in the saucepan boils, add the pasta along with a tablespoon of salt and give the pasta a quick stir. Briefly put the lid on until it starts to lift, showing that the water has come back to the boil, then let the pasta bubble away, uncovered, for about 8 minutes, or until it is tender but still has some bite to it.

4 Drain the pasta by tipping it all into a colander placed in the sink, then put it back into the still-warm pan. Either add the olive oil to the pasta, serve it onto warm plates and spoon the sauce on top; or add the sauce directly to the pasta, toss gently and serve onto warm plates. Garnish with fresh oregano and hand round the Parmesan.

FARFALLE WITH LENTIL BOLOGNESE SAUCE AND SPINACH Serves ❹

INGREDIENTS

400g / 14oz farfalle

salt

olive oil

225g / 8oz tender spinach

1 quantity of lentil bolognese sauce (page 100)

freshly ground black pepper

fresh Parmesan cheese, cut in flakes or grated, to serve

Spinach and lentils go together like bread and cheese or strawberries and cream ... Put together with pasta, spinach and lentils make a wonderfully filling and tasty dish.

1 Fill a large saucepan with 4 litres / 7 pints of water and put it on the stove to heat up for the pasta.

2 When the water boils, add the pasta along with a tablespoon of salt and give the pasta a quick stir. Briefly put the lid on until it starts to lift, showing that the water has come back to the boil, then let the pasta bubble away, uncovered, for about 8 minutes, or until it is tender but still has some bite to it.

3 Meanwhile, heat 1 tablespoon of olive oil in a saucepan, then add the spinach and stir-fry over a high heat for 1–2 minutes, until the spinach has wilted. Remove from the heat and drain off any liquid.

4 Add the spinach to the bolognese sauce in a pan and heat through gently. Check the seasoning, adding salt and pepper to taste if it needs it.

5 Drain the pasta by tipping it all into a colander placed in the sink, then put it back into the still-warm pan. Either add 1 tablespoon of olive oil to the pasta, serve it onto warm plates and spoon the sauce on top; or add the sauce directly to the pasta, toss gently and serve onto warm plates. Scatter the Parmesan on top and serve at once.

TOMATO SAUCE Serves 4

INGREDIENTS

1 tablespoon olive oil

1 onion, peeled and chopped

2 garlic cloves, peeled and crushed

2 x 400g / 14oz cans tomatoes in juice

salt and freshly ground black pepper

A wonderful, basic standby, tomato sauce is quick to make and popular with most people. This is my favourite recipe for it – and also one of the simplest.

1 Heat the oil in a large saucepan and add the onion. Cover and cook gently for 10 minutes, until tender but not brown.

2 Add the garlic, stir well and cook for 1–2 minutes longer. Then stir in the tomatoes, together with their juice, breaking up the tomatoes with a wooden spoon.

3 Bring to the boil, then let the mixture simmer for 10–15 minutes until the liquid has disappeared and the sauce is thick.

4 Season with salt and pepper – it is important to season a tomato sauce with salt after it has cooked because salt added during cooking can toughen tomatoes.

•

For this delicate and delectable variation, use 900g / 2lb fresh tomatoes, skinned and roughly chopped, instead of the canned tomatoes. Some fresh basil leaves, if available, torn into the sauce just before serving, make the perfect finishing touch.

PENNE WITH TOMATO SAUCE, CHILLI AND RED BEANS Serves 4

INGREDIENTS

400g / 14oz penne

salt

1 dried red chilli, crumbled, or 1 fresh green chilli, finely sliced

a 420g / 15oz can red kidney beans, drained

1 quantity of tomato sauce (above)

freshly ground black pepper

squeeze of lemon juice, optional

1 tablespoon olive oil, optional

several good sprigs of fresh coriander, to serve

This is a substantial dish, and particularly good on a chilly day. To make it even more filling you could serve it with warm bread, rolls or garlic bread.

1 Fill a large saucepan with 4 litres / 7 pints of water and put it on the stove to heat up for the pasta.

2 When the water boils, add the pasta along with a tablespoon of salt and give the pasta a quick stir. Briefly put the lid on until it starts to lift, showing that the water has come back to the boil, then let the pasta bubble away, uncovered, for about 8 minutes, or until it is tender but still has some bite to it.

3 Meanwhile, add the chilli and beans to the tomato sauce in a pan and heat through gently, stirring from time to time. Check the seasoning, adding pepper, a squeeze of lemon juice and salt to taste if it needs it.

4 Drain the pasta by tipping it all into a colander placed in the sink, then put it back into the still-warm pan. Either add the olive oil to the pasta, serve it onto warm plates and spoon the sauce on top; or add the sauce directly to the pasta, toss gently and serve onto warm plates. Chop, snip or tear the coriander over the top.

Penne with tomato sauce, chilli and red beans

RIGATONI WITH TOMATO SAUCE, AUBERGINES AND MOZZARELLA Serves ❹

INGREDIENTS

2 medium-sized aubergines

salt

400g / 14oz rigatoni

olive oil

1 quantity of tomato sauce (page 106)

freshly ground black pepper

225g / 8oz fresh mozzarella cheese, drained and cut into 6mm / ¼ inch cubes

fresh basil leaves and flakes of Parmesan cheese, to serve

You do not have to salt the aubergines in advance, but if you do, the aubergine will absorb less oil when you fry or grill it.

1 Cut the aubergines into thin slices. Sprinkle the slices with salt, put them into a colander and leave to drain for about an hour. Then rinse them under the cold tap and pat dry.

2 Fill a large saucepan with 4 litres / 7 pints of water and put it on the stove to heat up for the pasta.

3 When the water boils, add the pasta along with a tablespoon of salt and give the pasta a quick stir. Briefly put the lid on until it starts to lift, showing that the water has come back to the boil, then let the pasta bubble away, uncovered, for about 8 minutes, or until it is tender but still has some bite to it.

4 Meanwhile, heat a little olive oil in a frying pan and fry the aubergine slices until golden brown and tender; drain and blot

on kitchen paper. You will need to do more than one batch. Keep the aubergine slices warm under the grill. Alternatively, brush the slices of aubergine with oil and put them under a hot grill until they are tender and browned, turning them half-way through.

5 Heat the tomato sauce through gently. Check the seasoning, adding more – especially pepper – if it needs it. Stir two thirds of the mozzarella into the hot sauce so that it starts to melt.

6 Drain the pasta by tipping it all into a colander placed in the sink, then put it back into the still-warm pan. Either add the olive oil to the pasta, serve it onto warm plates and spoon the sauce on top; or add the sauce directly to the pasta, toss gently and serve onto warm plates. In either case, top each portion with some of the aubergine and the remaining mozzarella. Tear basil leaves over the top, scatter with flakes of Parmesan, and serve at once.

RUOTE DI CARRO WITH TOMATO SAUCE, SUN-DRIED TOMATOES AND COURGETTES Serves ❹

INGREDIENTS

400g / 14oz ruote di carro

salt

450g / 1lb courgettes, cut into 6mm / ¼ inch slices

2 tablespoons of oil from the sun-dried tomatoes, optional (see below)

freshly ground black pepper

8 sun-dried tomatoes, chopped

1 quantity of tomato sauce (page 106)

squeeze of lemon juice, optional

1 tablespoon olive oil, optional

fresh basil leaves and flakes of Parmesan cheese, to serve

Added sun-dried tomatoes intensify the flavour of the sauce and go well with the courgettes. This is also good made with farfalle or orecchiette – indeed any of the chunky pastas.

1 Fill a large saucepan with 4 litres / 7 pints of water and put it on the stove to heat up for the pasta.

2 When the water boils, add the pasta along with a tablespoon of salt and give the pasta a quick stir. Briefly put the lid on until it starts to lift, showing that the water has come back to the boil, then let the pasta bubble away, uncovered, for about 8 minutes, or until it is tender but still has some bite to it.

3 Meanwhile, cook the courgettes, either by sautéing in the oil from the sun-dried tomatoes or, for a less rich result, in a little boiling water. Either way they will take 3–4 minutes. Drain the courgettes if necessary, season with salt and pepper and keep them warm.

4 Add the sun-dried tomatoes to the tomato sauce in a pan and heat through gently. Check the seasoning, adding a squeeze of lemon juice to taste if it needs it.

5 Drain the pasta by tipping it all into a colander placed in the sink, then put it back into the still-warm pan. Either add the olive oil to the pasta, serve it onto warm plates and spoon the sauce on top; or add the sauce directly to the pasta, toss gently and serve onto warm plates. Top with the courgettes and some grindings of black pepper, then tear basil leaves over the top, scatter with flakes of Parmesan and serve at once.

•

Sun-dried tomatoes can be bought in oil, as a purée, or simply in their dried state. The ones in oil, and the purée, can be used as they are.

Dry sun-dried tomatoes need soaking for 30–60 minutes in hot water to plump them up, after which they can be used in the same way as tomatoes in oil. After soaking, they keep for no more than a day or two in the refrigerator, because they lack the protective layer of oil. They are, of course, low in fat, which can be an advantage.

PIPE RIGATE WITH TOMATO SAUCE, ARTICHOKE HEARTS AND SUN-DRIED TOMATOES Serves ❹

INGREDIENTS

400g / 14oz pipe rigate

salt

a 400g / 14oz can artichoke
hearts, drained and sliced

8 sun-dried tomatoes, chopped

1 quantity of tomato sauce (page 106)

freshly ground black pepper

squeeze of lemon juice, optional

1 tablespoon olive oil, optional

fresh basil leaves and flakes of
Parmesan cheese, to serve

This is one of my favourite mixtures; I like to serve it with a leafy salad with a light vinaigrette dressing.

1 Fill a large saucepan with 4 litres / 7 pints of water and put it on the stove to heat up for the pasta.

2 When the water boils, add the pasta along with a tablespoon of salt and give the pasta a quick stir. Briefly put the lid on until it starts to lift, showing that the water has come back to the boil, then let the pasta bubble away, uncovered, for about 8 minutes, or until it is tender but still has some bite to it.

3 Meanwhile, add the artichoke hearts and the sun-dried tomatoes to the tomato sauce in a pan and heat through gently. Check the seasoning, adding pepper, a squeeze of lemon juice and salt to taste if it needs it.

4 Drain the pasta by tipping it all into a colander placed in the sink, then put it back into the still-warm pan. Either add the olive oil to the pasta, serve it onto warm plates and spoon the sauce on top; or add the sauce directly to the pasta, toss gently and serve onto warm plates. Tear basil leaves over the top, scatter with flakes of Parmesan and serve at once.

SPAGHETTI WITH GINGER—TOMATO SAUCE, CHICKPEAS AND FRESH CORIANDER Serves ❹

INGREDIENTS

400g / 14oz spaghetti

salt

walnut-sized piece of fresh
ginger, grated

a 400g / 14oz can chickpeas, drained

1 quantity of tomato sauce
(page 106)

freshly ground black pepper

squeeze of lemon juice, optional

1 tablespoon olive oil, optional

several good sprigs of fresh
coriander

Here the classic combination of pasta and chickpeas is enlivened with a ginger—tomato sauce and coriander, to give the dish a slightly eastern flavour.

1 Fill a large saucepan with 4 litres / 7 pints of water and put it on the stove to heat up for the pasta.

2 When the water boils, add the spaghetti, holding it straight up like a bunch of flowers and gently pushing it into the water as it softens. Add a tablespoon of salt and give the pasta a quick stir. Briefly put the lid on until it starts to lift, showing that the water has come back to the boil, then let the pasta bubble away, uncovered, for about 8 minutes, or until it is tender but still has some bite to it.

3 Meanwhile, stir the ginger and chickpeas into the tomato sauce in a pan, and heat through gently. Just before the pasta is ready, check the seasoning of the sauce, adding pepper, a squeeze of lemon juice and salt to taste if it needs it.

4 Drain the pasta by tipping it all into a colander placed in the sink, then put it back into the still-warm pan. Either add the olive oil to the pasta, serve it onto warm plates and spoon the sauce on top; or add the sauce directly to the pasta, toss gently and serve onto warm plates. Chop, snip or tear the coriander over the top.

Pipe rigate with tomato
sauce, artichoke hearts
and sun-dried tomatoes

111

FARFALLE IN FRESH TOMATO SAUCE WITH FRESH BASIL Serves ❹

INGREDIENTS

400g / 14oz farfalle

salt

1 quantity of tomato sauce (page 106), made with fresh tomatoes

squeeze of lemon juice, optional

1 tablespoon olive oil, optional

freshly ground black pepper

fresh basil leaves

So simple but, when well made, unbeatable.

1 Fill a large saucepan with 4 litres / 7 pints of water and put it on the stove to heat up for the pasta.

2 When the water boils, add the pasta along with a tablespoon of salt and give the pasta a quick stir. Briefly put the lid on until it starts to lift, showing that the water has come back to the boil, then let the pasta bubble away, uncovered, for about 8 minutes, or until it is tender but still has some bite to it.

3 Heat the tomato sauce through gently. Check the seasoning, adding a squeeze of lemon juice to taste if it needs it.

4 Drain the pasta by tipping it all into a colander placed in the sink, then put it back into the still-warm pan. Either add the olive oil to the pasta, serve it onto warm plates and spoon the sauce on top; or add the sauce directly to the pasta, toss gently and serve onto warm plates. Grind a little pepper coarsely on top, tear the basil leaves over and serve at once.

LASAGNETTE WITH FRESH TOMATO SAUCE, GRILLED GOLDEN PEPPERS AND OLIVES Serves ❹

INGREDIENTS

2 large golden peppers

400g / 14oz lasagnette

salt

1 quantity of tomato sauce (page 106)

125g / 4oz black olives

freshly ground black pepper

1 tablespoon olive oil, optional

fresh basil leaves, to serve

Another mixture of ingredients which seems to go well with almost any type of pasta, especially chunky ones. Use red peppers instead of the golden ones, if you prefer.

1 Fill a large saucepan with 4 litres / 7 pints of water and put it on the stove to heat up for the pasta.

2 Meanwhile, prepare the peppers by cutting them into quarters and placing, skin-side (shiny-side) up, on a grill pan. Put under a high heat for 10–15 minutes, until the skin has blistered and blackened in places. Cover the peppers with a plate and leave until cool enough to handle, then remove the skin, stem and seeds, and cut the flesh into slices. Keep the slices warm.

3 When the water in the saucepan boils, add the pasta along with a tablespoon of salt and give the pasta a quick stir. Briefly put the lid on until it starts to lift, showing that the water has come back to the boil, then let the pasta bubble away, uncovered, for about 8 minutes, or until it is tender but still has some bite to it.

4 Heat the tomato sauce through gently. Add the olives and check the seasoning, adding pepper to taste if it needs it.

5 Drain the pasta by tipping it all into a colander placed in the sink, then put it back into the still-warm pan. Either add the olive oil to the pasta, serve it onto warm plates and spoon the sauce on top; or add the sauce directly to the pasta, toss gently and serve onto warm plates. Top with the golden pepper and tear the basil leaves over.

LASAGNETTE WITH MASCARPONE AND MUSHROOMS IN TOMATO SAUCE Serves ❹

INGREDIENTS

400g / 14oz lasagnette

salt

25g / 1oz butter

450g / 1lb mushrooms, washed and sliced

2 garlic cloves, peeled and crushed

125g / 4oz mascarpone cheese (or you could use a low-fat cream cheese)

1 quantity of tomato sauce (page 106)

freshly ground black pepper

1 tablespoon olive oil, optional

fresh basil leaves and flakes of Parmesan cheese, to serve

I like frilly lasagnette for this, but if it is unavailable, substitute almost any other pasta that you fancy, long or short. This is a very easy-going mixture and does not depend on any particular type of pasta for flavour or effect.

1 Fill a large saucepan with 4 litres / 7 pints of water and put it on the stove to heat up for the pasta.

2 When the water boils, add the pasta along with a tablespoon of salt and give the pasta a quick stir. Briefly put the lid on until it starts to lift, showing that the water has come back to the boil, then let the pasta bubble away, uncovered, for about 8 minutes, or until it is tender but still has some bite to it.

3 Meanwhile, cook the mushrooms: melt the butter in a medium saucepan, add the mushrooms and garlic and cook for 4–5 minutes, or until they are tender and any liquid has disappeared, stirring from time to time.

4 Add the mascarpone cheese to the tomato sauce in a pan and heat through gently, stirring until the cheese has melted. Then add the mushrooms and check the seasoning, adding salt and pepper to taste if it needs it.

5 Drain the pasta by tipping it all into a colander placed in the sink, then put it back into the still-warm pan. Either add the olive oil to the pasta, serve it onto warm plates and spoon the sauce on top; or add the sauce directly to the pasta, toss gently and serve onto warm plates. Tear some basil leaves over, scatter with flakes of Parmesan and serve as soon as possible.

RIGATONI WITH TOMATO SAUCE, GRILLED FENNEL AND OLIVES Serves ❹

INGREDIENTS

450g / 1lb fennel bulbs, trimmed, reserving any feathery leaves, and sliced into eighths

olive oil

400g / 14oz rigatoni

salt

1 quantity of tomato sauce (page 106)

freshly ground black pepper

squeeze of lemon juice, optional

125g / 4oz black olives

Juicy slices of grilled fennel combine well with the tomato sauce and olives. Serve this with some warm crusty bread.

1 Fill a large saucepan with 4 litres / 7 pints of water and put it on the stove to heat up for the pasta.

2 Meanwhile, par-boil the fennel in a little boiling water for 4–5 minutes, until just tender, and then drain well. Brush the fennel lightly all over with olive oil, put it in a single layer on a grill pan or baking sheet that will fit under your grill, and grill under a high heat until tender and tinged with brown: 4–5 minutes. Keep the fennel warm.

3 When the water in the saucepan boils, add the pasta along with a tablespoon of salt and give the pasta a quick stir. Briefly put the lid on until it starts to lift, showing that the water has come back to the boil, then let the pasta bubble away, uncovered, for about 8 minutes, or until it is tender but still has some bite to it.

4 Heat the tomato sauce through gently. Check the seasoning, adding pepper, a squeeze of lemon juice and salt to taste if it needs it.

5 Drain the pasta by tipping it all into a colander placed in the sink, then put it back into the still-warm pan, then either add 1 tablespoon of olive oil to the pasta, serve it onto warm plates and spoon the sauce on top; or add the sauce directly to the pasta, toss gently and serve onto warm plates. Either way, top with the grilled fennel and black olives and serve at once.

SPAGHETTI PUTTANESCA Serves ❹

INGREDIENTS

400g / 14oz spaghetti

salt

1 quantity of tomato sauce
(page 106)

2 garlic cloves, peeled and crushed

1 tablespoon sun-dried tomato purée

2 tablespoons capers

50g / 2oz pitted black olives, sliced

1 teaspoon chopped fresh oregano

freshly ground black pepper

1 tablespoon olive oil, optional

Well known but none the less delicious, this 'whore's pasta' is spicy and piquant.

1 Fill a large saucepan with 4 litres / 7 pints of water and put it on the stove to heat up for the pasta.

2 When the water boils, add the spaghetti, holding it straight up like a bunch of flowers and gently pushing it into the water as it softens. Add a tablespoon of salt and give the pasta a quick stir. Briefly put the lid on until it starts to lift, showing that the water has come back to the boil, then let the pasta bubble away, uncovered, for about 8 minutes, or until it is tender but still has some bite to it.

3 Meanwhile, add the garlic, sun-dried tomato purée, capers, olives and oregano to the tomato sauce in a pan and heat through gently, stirring from time to time. Check the seasoning, adding more – especially pepper – if you think it needs it.

4 Drain the pasta by tipping it all into a colander placed in the sink, then put it back into the still-warm pan. Either add the olive oil to the pasta, serve it onto warm plates and spoon the sauce on top; or add the sauce directly to the pasta, toss gently and serve onto warm plates.

PENNE ARRABBIATA Serves ❹

INGREDIENTS

400g / 14oz penne

salt

1 dried red chilli, crumbled

1 tablespoon sun-dried tomato purée

1 quantity of tomato sauce
(page 106)

freshly ground black pepper

1 tablespoon olive oil, optional

A lovely, punchy, classic pasta dish; you can vary the heat by adding more or less chilli.

1 Fill a large saucepan with 4 litres / 7 pints of water and put it on the stove to heat up for the pasta.

2 When the water boils, add the pasta along with a tablespoon of salt and give the pasta a quick stir. Briefly put the lid on until it starts to lift, showing that the water has come back to the boil, then let the pasta bubble away, uncovered, for about 8 minutes, or until it is tender but still has some bite to it.

3 Meanwhile, add the red chilli and the sun-dried tomato purée to the tomato sauce in a pan and heat through gently, stirring from time to time. Check the seasoning, adding salt and pepper to taste if it needs it.

4 Drain the pasta by tipping it all into a colander placed in the sink, then put it back into the still-warm pan. Either add the olive oil to the pasta, serve it onto warm plates and spoon the sauce on top; or add the sauce directly to the pasta, toss gently and serve onto warm plates.

CONCHIGLIE WITH SWEETCORN AND TOMATO SAUCE Serves ❹

INGREDIENTS

400g / 14oz conchiglie

salt

225g / 8oz sweetcorn, cut from the cob, frozen or canned

1 quantity of tomato sauce (page 106)

freshly ground black pepper

squeeze of lemon juice, optional

1 tablespoon olive oil, optional

A simple mixture that is popular with children. You can use fresh, frozen or canned sweetcorn. I like to serve it with salad; a mixture of grated carrot and shredded cabbage, lightly dressed, is also well liked by children.

1 Fill a large saucepan with 4 litres / 7 pints of water and put it on the stove to heat up for the pasta.

2 When the water boils, add the pasta along with a tablespoon of salt and give the pasta a quick stir. Briefly put the lid on until it starts to lift, showing that the water has come back to the boil, then let the pasta bubble away, uncovered, for about 8 minutes, or until it is tender but still has some bite to it.

3 Meanwhile, cook the sweetcorn in a little boiling water for 3–4 minutes, or until it is just tender, then drain and add to the tomato sauce in a pan.

4 Heat the tomato sauce through gently. Check the seasoning, adding pepper, a squeeze of lemon juice and salt to taste if it needs it.

5 Drain the pasta by tipping it all into a colander placed in the sink, then put it back into the still-warm pan. Either add the olive oil to the pasta, serve it onto warm plates and spoon the sauce on top; or add the sauce directly to the pasta, toss gently and serve onto warm plates.

FUSILLI WITH CREAMY TOMATO SAUCE, PEAS, BASIL AND PARMESAN Serves ❹

INGREDIENTS

400g / 14oz fusilli

salt

450g / 1lb podded fresh peas or frozen petits pois

1 quantity of tomato sauce (page 106)

4 tablespoons single cream

freshly ground black pepper

1 tablespoon olive oil, optional

fresh basil leaves and flakes of Parmesan cheese

The cream reduces the acidity of the sauce, making this a very mellow dish. Soya cream also works well.

1 Fill a large saucepan with 4 litres / 7 pints of water and put it on the stove to heat up for the pasta.

2 When the water boils, add the pasta along with a tablespoon of salt and give the pasta a quick stir. Briefly put the lid on until it starts to lift, showing that the water has come back to the boil, then let the pasta bubble away, uncovered, for about 8 minutes, or until it is tender but still has some bite to it.

3 Add the peas to the tomato sauce in a pan and place over a gentle heat, to heat through both the peas and the sauce. Just before the pasta is done, add the cream to the sauce and check the seasoning, adding salt and pepper to taste if it needs it.

4 Drain the pasta by tipping it all into a colander placed in the sink, then put it back into the still-warm pan. Either add the olive oil to the pasta, serve it onto warm plates and spoon the sauce on top; or add the sauce directly to the pasta, toss gently and serve onto warm plates. Tear basil leaves over the top, scatter with Parmesan and serve at once.

Lasagne and other Baked Pasta Dishes

This section contains a variety of dishes linked by the fact that after they have been assembled they need to be baked in the oven or cooked under the grill. Some of them are quite simple, others take a bit longer to put together. The hard work can often be done well in advance, however, making many of them perfect for informal entertaining.

Anyone who has had to cater for a crowd will know the advantages of dishes such as lasagne – you can make them in advance, bake them when you are ready and know that they will not spoil if the meal is a little delayed. So I have included a good selection of different types of lasagne, some of which are a little out of the ordinary. They all freeze well, too. Freeze them before baking, and remember to get them out of the freezer the night before to allow time to thaw.

Pasta bakes serve a rather similar function to lasagne and make a nice variation on that theme. These freeze well, too and, like lasagne, need only be accompanied by a salad or a very simple cooked vegetable such as green beans or spinach. Again, they make a practical choice for feeding a crowd. One of the more unusual pasta bakes is the terrine, which is easy to make and stunning to look at. It is good either as a starter or a light main course.

Also included in this section are some vegetable dishes in which pasta is used to make a tasty stuffing, and some delicious cannelloni bakes.

RED BEAN LASAGNE Serves ❻

INGREDIENTS

1 tablespoon olive oil
1 onion, peeled and very finely chopped
1 large garlic clove, peeled and crushed
a 400g / 14oz can tomatoes
2 x 420g / 15oz cans red kidney beans, drained and rinsed
2 heaped tablespoons sun-dried tomato purée
½–1 teaspoon chilli powder
salt and freshly ground black pepper
150–175g / 5–6oz oven-ready lasagne verde
1 quantity of béchamel sauce (page 90)
50g / 2oz freshly grated Parmesan cheese

This moist and delicious lasagne is high in protein thanks to its ideal pasta-and-pulse combination. It is good with a leafy salad or a lightly cooked vegetable, such as green beans or broccoli.

1 Set the oven to 200°C/400°F/gas 6. Grease a casserole dish or roasting tin about 20 x 30cm / 8 x 12 inches and at least 6cm / 2½ inches deep.

2 Heat the oil in a medium-sized saucepan and fry the onion for 5 minutes with a lid on the pan. Then add the garlic and cook for a few seconds longer. Add the tomatoes, breaking them up with a wooden spoon, and then the red kidney beans. Bring to the boil, then leave to simmer, uncovered, for 10–15 minutes, until thick. Add the sun-dried tomato purée, chilli powder and salt and pepper to taste.

3 Rinse the ready-to-use lasagne sheets under the cold tap, then arrange sheets of lasagne in the base of the dish, to cover it. On top of this put a layer of béchamel sauce, then half the red bean mixture. Top this with another layer of lasagne, then half of the remaining béchamel and the rest of the red kidney bean mixture. Finish with a layer of lasagne followed by the remainder of the béchamel sauce. Scatter the Parmesan cheese on top.

4 Bake the lasagne for 35–40 minutes, until the pasta is tender and the top golden brown.

SPINACH LASAGNE Serves ❻

INGREDIENTS

50g / 2oz butter
700g / 1½lb frozen spinach, thawed, or fresh spinach, washed
225g / 8oz ricotta cheese
2 garlic cloves, peeled and crushed
125g / 4oz freshly grated Parmesan cheese
freshly grated nutmeg
salt and freshly ground black pepper
150–175g / 5–6oz oven-ready lasagne
1 quantity of béchamel sauce (page 90)

I am always making different versions of this lasagne because it is so popular with my daughter and her friends. This is my latest.

1 Set the oven to 200°C/400°F/gas 6. Grease a casserole dish or roasting tin about 20 x 30cm / 8 x 12 inches and at least 6cm / 2 ½ inches deep.

2 Melt the butter in a large saucepan and put in the spinach. Cook for 5–6 minutes, or until the spinach is tender, pushing it down and chopping it with the end of a fish slice or spatula. Unless you have a very large saucepan you may need to do the spinach in two batches, using half the butter each time.

3 Mix the spinach with the ricotta cheese, garlic, half the Parmesan, and nutmeg, salt and pepper to taste.

4 To assemble the lasagne, rinse the ready-to-use lasagne sheets under the cold tap, then arrange half of the sheets of lasagne in the base of the dish, to cover it. Pour in a little of the béchamel sauce. Put in half the spinach mixture, another layer of béchamel sauce and then the remaining spinach. Follow with the remaining lasagne and the rest of the béchamel. Scatter the rest of the Parmesan on top.

5 Bake the lasagne for 35–40 minutes, until the pasta is tender and the top golden brown.

VEGETARIAN LASAGNE AL FORNO Serves ❻

Based on a recipe I created for my book *The New Simply Delicious*, this is a vegetarian version of the classic Lasagne al Forno which does not use lentils to replace the meat but rather a light and tasty mushroom sauce. A delectable dish.

INGREDIENTS

150–175g / 5–6oz oven-ready lasagne verde

1 quantity of béchamel sauce (page 90)

50g / 2oz freshly grated Parmesan cheese

FOR THE MUSHROOM BOLOGNESE SAUCE:

2 tablespoons olive oil

1 onion, peeled and very finely chopped

450g / 1lb mushrooms

1 large garlic clove, peeled and crushed

a 400g / 14oz can tomatoes

2 tablespoons sherry or 3–4 tablespoons red wine

2 heaped tablespoons sun-dried tomato purée

1 teaspoon dried basil

2 teaspoons black olive paste or pitted and mashed black olives

salt and freshly ground black pepper

1 Set the oven to 200°C/400°F/gas 6. Grease a casserole dish or roasting tin about 20 x 30cm / 8 x 12 inches and at least 6cm / 2½ inches deep.

2 Make the mushroom bolognese sauce: heat the oil in a medium-sized saucepan and fry the onion for 5 minutes with a lid on the pan. Meanwhile, wipe the mushrooms with a clean damp cloth, then chop them up as finely as possible – they can be done in a food processor, but take care not to purée them completely.

3 Add the mushrooms to the onion along with the garlic (if you are chopping the mushrooms in a food processor the whole peeled garlic clove can be crushed by putting it in with them) and fry for a further 5 minutes, browning lightly and stirring often.

4 Add the tomatoes, sherry or wine, sun-dried tomato purée and basil. Mix well, then put a lid on the pan and leave the sauce to simmer for 25–30 minutes, until thick. Add the olive paste and salt and pepper to taste.

5 Rinse the ready-to-use lasagne sheets under the cold tap, then arrange sheets of lasagne in the base of the dish, to cover it. On top of this put first a layer of half the mushroom sauce, then one of béchamel sauce, using a third of the sauce. Top this with another layer of lasagne, then the rest of the mushroom sauce followed by béchamel. Finish with a layer of lasagne followed by the remainder of the béchamel. Scatter the Parmesan on top.

6 Bake the lasagne for 35–40 minutes, until the pasta is tender and the top golden brown.

SWEETCORN, RICOTTA, TOMATO AND CHEDDAR CHEESE LASAGNE Serves ❻

INGREDIENTS

450g / 1lb ricotta cheese

300g / 10oz frozen or canned sweetcorn

125g / 4oz Cheddar cheese, grated

salt and freshly ground black pepper

150–175g / 5–6oz oven-ready lasagne verde

2 x quantity of tomato sauce (page 106)

Another dish that is popular with the younger age group, and quite quick to make.

1 Set the oven to 200°C/400°F/gas 6. Grease a casserole dish or roasting tin about 20 x 30cm / 8 x 12 inches and at least 6cm / 2½ inches deep.

2 Mix the ricotta cheese with the sweetcorn (no need to cook it) and half the cheese. Season with salt and pepper.

3 To assemble the lasagne, rinse the ready-to-use lasagne sheets under the cold tap, then arrange sheets of lasagne in the base of the dish, to cover it. Pour in a little of the tomato sauce. Put in half the sweetcorn mixture, then another layer of lasagne and some more tomato sauce. Follow with the rest of the sweetcorn mixture, the remaining lasagne and the rest of the tomato sauce. Scatter the remaining Cheddar cheese on top.

4 Bake the lasagne for 35–40 minutes, until the pasta is tender and the top golden brown.

MUSHROOM AND GARLIC CREAM CHEESE LASAGNE Serves ❻

INGREDIENTS

2 tablespoons olive oil

1 onion, peeled and finely chopped

700g / 1½lb mushrooms, washed and sliced

1 large garlic clove, peeled and crushed

225g / 8oz full-fat or reduced fat garlic cream cheese

salt and freshly ground black pepper

150–175g / 5–6oz oven-ready lasagne verde

2 x quantity of tomato sauce (page 106)

50g / 2oz freshly grated Parmesan cheese

A mixed salad goes well with this lasagne; vary the types of mushroom used if you can get hold of some exciting ones.

1 Set the oven to 200°C/400°F/gas 6. Grease a casserole dish or roasting tin about 20 x 30cm / 8 x 12 inches and at least 6cm / 2½ inches deep.

2 Heat the oil in a medium-sized saucepan and fry the onion for 5 minutes with a lid on the pan. Then add the sliced mushrooms to the onion along with the garlic and fry for a further 5–10 minutes, until the mushrooms are tender and any liquid they have produced has boiled away. Remove the pan from the heat, stir in the cream cheese and season with salt and pepper.

3 Rinse the ready-to-use lasagne sheets under the cold tap, then arrange sheets of lasagne in the base of the dish, to cover it. On top of this put first a layer of tomato sauce, then half the mushroom sauce, followed by a layer of lasagne and another of tomato sauce. Top this with the remaining mushroom mixture, the rest of the lasagne and a final layer of tomato sauce. Scatter the Parmesan cheese on top.

4 Bake the lasagne for 35–40 minutes, until the pasta is tender and the top golden brown.

ROASTED ASPARAGUS AND FRESH HERB LASAGNE Serves ❻

INGREDIENTS

2 bunches of asparagus, tough ends removed and the spears cut in half

2 tablespoons olive oil

4 tablespoons chopped fresh herbs: parsley, chervil, chives

salt and freshly ground black pepper

150–175g / 5–6oz oven-ready lasagne

1 quantity of béchamel sauce (page 90)

50g / 2oz freshly grated Parmesan cheese

This lasagne is light and fresh; just right with a summery salad of young vegetables and some chilled white wine.

1 Set the oven to 200°C/400°F/gas 6. Grease a casserole dish or roasting tin about 20 x 30cm / 8 x 12 inches and at least 6cm / 2½ inches deep.

2 Toss the asparagus in the oil, using your fingers to make sure that each piece is coated. Put the asparagus into a shallow roasting tin and roast in the oven for 20 minutes. Then remove from the oven and add the herbs and salt and pepper to taste.

3 Rinse the ready-to-use lasagne sheets under the cold tap, then arrange sheets of lasagne in the base of the dish, to cover it. On top of this put first a layer of béchamel sauce, then half the asparagus followed by a layer of lasagne and more cream sauce. Top this with the rest of the asparagus. Finish with a layer of lasagne followed by the remainder of the béchamel sauce and scatter the Parmesan cheese on top.

4 Bake the lasagne for 35–40 minutes, until the pasta is tender and the top golden brown.

RED ONION AND GOAT'S CHEESE LASAGNE Serves ❻

INGREDIENTS

2 tablespoons olive oil

25g / 1oz butter

700g / 1½lb red onions, peeled and sliced

1 large garlic clove, peeled and crushed

salt and freshly ground black pepper

150–175g / 5–6oz oven-ready lasagne verde

1 quantity of béchamel sauce (page 90)

200g / 7oz goat's cheese log, sliced into thin rounds

Warming and good for winter, this lasagne can also be made with ordinary onions instead of the red ones. The important thing is to let them cook for long enough so that they become sweet and melting.

1 Set the oven to 200°C/400°F/gas 6. Grease a casserole dish or roasting tin about 20 x 30cm / 8 x 12 inches and at least 6cm / 2½ inches deep.

2 Heat the oil and butter in a large saucepan and fry the onions and garlic gently for 30 minutes, until they are very tender, stirring from time to time. Season with salt and freshly ground black pepper.

3 Rinse the ready-to-use lasagne sheets under the cold tap, then arrange sheets of lasagne in the base of the dish, to cover it. On top of this put first a layer of béchamel sauce, then half the onions. Top this with another layer of lasagne, then more béchamel sauce, a layer of half of the goat's cheese and the rest of the onions. Finish with a layer of lasagne followed by the remainder of the béchamel and the rest of the goat's cheese.

4 Bake the lasagne for 35–40 minutes, until the pasta is tender and the top golden brown.

BROCCOLI AND BRIE LASAGNE Serves ❻

INGREDIENTS

700g / 1½lb prepared broccoli, cut into small pieces

salt and freshly ground black pepper

150–175g / 5–6oz oven-ready lasagne

1 quantity of béchamel sauce (page 90), or 2 x tomato sauce (page 106)

200g / 7oz Brie cheese, thinly sliced

Serve this with a tomato salad, or some roasted tomatoes that can be done in the oven with the lasagne.

1 Set the oven to 200°C/400°F/gas 6. Grease a casserole dish or roasting tin about 20 x 30cm / 8 x 12 inches and at least 6cm / 2½ inches deep.

2 Cook the broccoli in a little boiling water for 4–5 minutes until it is tender; drain and season with salt and pepper.

3 Rinse the ready-to-use lasagne sheets under the cold tap, then arrange sheets of lasagne in the base of the dish, to cover it. On top of this put first a layer of sauce, then half the broccoli. Top this with another layer of lasagne, then more sauce, a layer of half of the Brie cheese and the rest of the broccoli. Finish with a layer of lasagne followed by the remainder of the sauce and the rest of the Brie cheese.

4 Bake the lasagne for 35–40 minutes, until the pasta is tender and the top golden brown.

LEEK, OLIVE, FETA AND SUN-DRIED TOMATO LASAGNE Serves ❻

INGREDIENTS

700g / 1½lb leeks, trimmed and cut into 6mm / ¼ inch slices

2 tablespoons oil from the sun-dried tomatoes, optional

50g / 2oz sun-dried tomatoes, chopped

50g / 2oz stoned and chopped black olives

1 tablespoon chopped fresh oregano, optional

salt and freshly ground black pepper

150–175g / 5–6oz oven-ready lasagne

1 quantity of béchamel sauce (page 90)

200g / 7oz feta cheese, thinly sliced

One of my favourite combinations of flavours and textures – leeks, sun-dried tomatoes and olives – is here in this lasagne. Good with a green salad.

1 Set the oven to 200°C/400°F/gas 6. Grease a casserole dish or roasting tin about 20 x 30cm / 8 x 12 inches and at least 6cm / 2½ inches deep.

2 Prepare the leeks, either by sautéing in the oil from the sun-dried tomatoes or, for a less rich result, by cooking in a little boiling water. Either way they will take about 6 minutes. Drain the leeks if necessary and add the sun-dried tomatoes, olives, oregano if using, and salt and pepper to taste.

3 Rinse the ready-to-use lasagne sheets under the cold tap, then arrange sheets of lasagne in the base of the dish, to cover it. On top of this put first a layer of béchamel sauce, then half the leek mixture. Top this with another layer of lasagne, then more sauce, a layer of half of the feta cheese and the rest of the leek mixture. Finish with a layer of lasagne followed by the remainder of the sauce and the rest of the feta cheese.

4 Bake the lasagne for 35–40 minutes, until the pasta is tender and the top golden brown.

PUMPKIN AND GOAT'S CHEESE LASAGNE Serves ❻

INGREDIENTS

2 tablespoons olive oil

25g / 1oz butter

1 onion, peeled and chopped

1.6kg / 3½lb pumpkin, skin and seeds removed, flesh cut into 1cm / ½ inch dice (weight after skin and seeds taken away about 1.1kg / 2½lb)

1 large garlic clove, peeled and crushed

salt and freshly ground black pepper

150–175g / 5–6oz oven-ready lasagne verde

1 quantity of béchamel sauce (page 90)

200g / 7oz goat's cheese log, sliced into thin rounds

An excellent combination of flavours and textures, this is a lovely lasagne for the cooler days of autumn. If you prefer, you can use a tomato sauce (see page 106) instead of the béchamel for a very colourful result.

1 Set the oven to 200°C/400°F/gas 6. Grease a casserole dish or roasting tin about 20 x 30cm / 8 x 12 inches and at least 6cm / 2½ inches deep.

2 Heat the oil and butter in a large saucepan and fry the onion gently for 5 minutes with a lid on the pan. Then add the pumpkin and garlic, and mix so that the pumpkin is coated with the butter and oil. Cover the pan and cook slowly for 15–20 minutes, until the pumpkin is tender. Season with salt and pepper.

3 Rinse the ready-to-use lasagne sheets under the cold tap, then arrange sheets of lasagne in the base of the dish, to cover it. On top of this put first a layer of béchamel sauce, then half the pumpkin. Top this with another layer of lasagne, then more béchamel sauce, a layer of half of the goat's cheese and the rest of the pumpkin. Finish with a layer of lasagne followed by the remainder of the béchamel and the rest of the goat's cheese.

4 Bake the lasagne for 35–40 minutes, until the pasta is tender and the top golden brown.

SPAGHETTI, TOMATO, CHEESE AND MUSHROOM BAKE Serves ❹

INGREDIENTS

175g / 6oz spaghetti

salt

1 tablespoon olive oil

1 onion, peeled and chopped

225g / 8oz mushrooms, washed and chopped

1 garlic clove, peeled and crushed

a 400g / 14oz can tomatoes

1 egg, beaten

125g / 4oz Cheddar or Gruyère cheese, grated

1 tablespoon chopped fresh oregano

freshly ground black pepper

25g / 1oz freshly grated Parmesan cheese

4 tablespoons fresh breadcrumbs

This is a good recipe for serving to a crowd. It can be made well in advance – particularly useful when you have a lot of guests.

1 Fill a large saucepan with 4 litres / 7 pints of water and put it on the stove to heat up for the pasta.

2 Set the oven to 200°C/400°F/gas 6. Grease a casserole dish or roasting tin about 20 x 30cm / 8 x 12 inches and at least 6cm / 2½ inches deep.

3 When the water in the saucepan boils, add the spaghetti, holding it straight up like a bunch of flowers and gently pushing it into the water as it softens. Add a tablespoon of salt and give the pasta a quick stir. Briefly put the lid on until it starts to lift, showing that the water has come back to the boil, then let the pasta bubble away, uncovered, for about 8 minutes, or until it is tender but still has some bite to it. Drain the spaghetti.

4 Meanwhile, heat the oil in a medium-sized saucepan and put in the onion; cover and cook for 5 minutes. Then add the mushrooms, garlic and tomatoes and cook, uncovered, for a further 10 minutes, until the onions and mushrooms are tender.

5 Add the egg to the vegetable mixture and stir well over the heat for a minute or two until the egg has cooked. Remove from the heat and add the spaghetti, along with the Cheddar or Gruyère cheese. Season with salt and pepper.

6 Spoon the spaghetti mixture into the ovenproof dish, scatter with the breadcrumbs and Parmesan cheese and bake for about 30 minutes, until golden brown and crisp on top.

MEDITERRANEAN BAKE WITH CONCHIGLIE Serves ❹

INGREDIENTS

2 tablespoons olive oil

1 onion, peeled and chopped

1 fennel bulb

1 garlic clove, peeled and crushed

1 red pepper, de-seeded and chopped

1 yellow pepper, de-seeded and chopped

a 400g / 14oz can tomatoes

225g / 8oz conchiglie

salt

50g / 2oz black olives, optional

freshly ground black pepper

125g / 4oz Gruyère cheese, grated

Another useful recipe that can be made in advance if you wish. In this case, it is best baked in the oven, to heat it through thoroughly. It needs about 30 minutes at 200°C/400°F/gas 6.

Serve with a leafy salad – for instance, baby spinach leaves and thinly sliced purple onions in a mustardy vinaigrette – and warm, crusty bread.

1 Fill a large saucepan with 4 litres / 7 pints of water and put it on the stove to heat up for the pasta.

2 Meanwhile, heat 1 tablespoon of the oil in a medium-sized saucepan and put in the onion; cover and cook for 5 minutes.

3 With a sharp knife, pare away any tough, outer layers of the fennel. Then slice the fennel and add to the onions, along with the garlic, red and yellow peppers and tomatoes. Cook, uncovered, for 15–20 minutes, or until all the vegetables are tender.

4 When the water in the saucepan boils, add the pasta along with a tablespoon of salt and give the pasta a quick stir. Briefly put the lid on until it starts to lift, showing that the water has come back to the boil, then let the pasta bubble away, uncovered, for about 8 minutes, or until it is tender but still has some bite to it.

5 Set the grill to high. Drain the pasta and put it into a shallow dish that will fit under the grill. Add the remaining tablespoon of olive oil and toss well.

6 Add the olives, if using, to the vegetable mixture, season the mixture with salt and pepper, and then pour this over the pasta. Top with a layer of Gruyère cheese, then place under the grill until the cheese has melted and is golden brown, and the dish is piping hot right through. Serve at once.

PASTA TERRINE Serves ❻ to ❽

An impressive dish that is very easy to make and serves 6 to 8 people. Serve it cold, in slices, on a pool of tomato sauce or with a mixture of mayonnaise, low-fat yogurt and green peppercorns. Or eat it hot, in thick slices, with lightly cooked vegetables or a crisp salad.

1 Fill a large saucepan with 4 litres / 7 pints of water and put it on the stove to heat up for the pasta.

2 Set the oven to 180°C/350°F/gas 4. Line a 900g / 2lb loaf tin with a strip of non-stick baking parchment to cover the base and extend up the narrow sides. Grease with butter.

3 When the water in the saucepan boils, add the pasta along with a tablespoon of salt and give the pasta a quick stir. Briefly put the lid on until it starts to lift, showing that the water has come back to the boil, then let the pasta bubble away, uncovered, for about 8 minutes, or until it is tender but still has some bite to it. Drain the pasta.

4 Meanwhile, heat the oil in a medium-sized saucepan and add the onion; cover and cook for 5 minutes. Then add the garlic, green pepper and tomatoes and cook, uncovered, for a further 10–15 minutes, until the onions and pepper are tender and the mixture is thick. Remove from the heat.

5 Add the pasta to the tomato mixture in the pan, along with the breadcrumbs, sun-dried tomato purée, oregano, eggs, three-quarters of the cheese, and salt and pepper to taste. Mix well, then pour into the loaf tin.

6 Scatter with the remaining Parmesan and bake for about 45 minutes, until the terrine is firm to the touch and a knife inserted into the centre comes out clean. Cool for a minute or two in the tin, then slip a knife around the edges, invert the tin over a plate and turn the terrine out. Serve in slices.

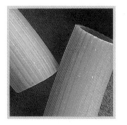

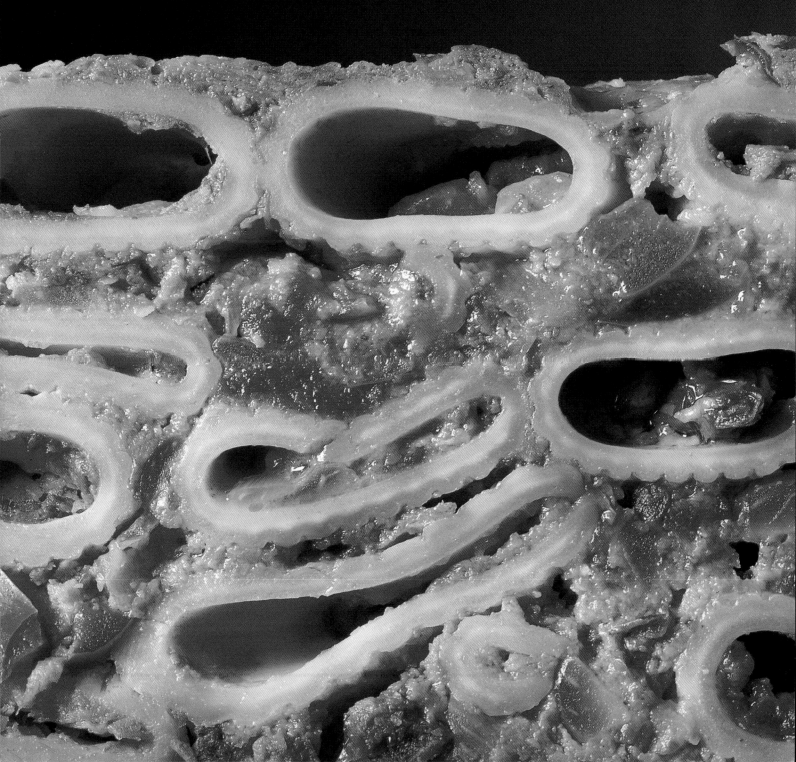

CHILLI PASTA BAKE WITH RED BEANS Serves ❹

INGREDIENTS

225g / 8oz penne

salt

2 tablespoons olive oil

1 onion, peeled and chopped

1 garlic clove, peeled and crushed

1 red pepper, de-seeded and chopped

a 400g / 14oz can tomatoes

a 420g / 15oz can red kidney beans, drained and rinsed

2 tablespoons sun-dried tomato purée

½–1 teaspoon chilli powder

freshly ground black pepper

50g / 2oz fresh breadcrumbs

This dish is useful when you want to make something ahead of time that is tasty and filling. Serve it with a salad of avocado and green leaves in a light vinaigrette dressing, and some bread or tortilla chips.

1 Fill a large saucepan with 4 litres / 7 pints of water and put it on the stove to heat up for the pasta.

2 Set the oven to 200°C/400°F/gas 6. Grease a casserole dish or roasting tin about 20 x 30cm / 8 x 12 inches and at least 6cm / 2½ inches deep.

3 When the water in the saucepan boils, add the pasta along with a tablespoon of salt and give the pasta a quick stir. Briefly put the lid on until it starts to lift, showing that the water has come back to the boil, then let the pasta bubble away, uncovered, for about 8 minutes, or until it is tender but still has some bite to it. Drain the pasta.

4 Meanwhile, heat 1 tablespoon of the oil in a medium-sized saucepan and put in the onion; cover and cook for minutes. Then add the garlic, red pepper, tomatoes and beans, and cook, uncovered, for a further 10–15 minutes, until the onions and pepper are tender and the mixture is thick. Remove from the heat.

5 Add the sun-dried tomato purée, then season the mixture with chilli powder to taste, salt and pepper. Add the pasta, and toss well in the sauce.

6 Spoon the mixture into the prepared dish. Mix the breadcrumbs with the remaining oil and scatter them on top. Bake for about 30 minutes, until the crumbs are browned and crisp.

PASTA, LENTIL AND VEGETABLE BAKE WITH FETA CHEESE AND THYME Serves ❹

INGREDIENTS

125g / 4oz green or brown lentils, or a 400g / 14oz can

125g / 4oz any small pasta: macaroni, penne, rigatoni

salt

2 tablespoons olive oil

1 onion, peeled and chopped

1 garlic clove, peeled and crushed

2 large carrots, peeled and cut into 6mm / ¼ inch slices

2 sticks of celery

225g / 8oz leeks, trimmed and cut into 6mm / ¼ inch slices

2 tablespoons sun-dried tomato purée

1 tablespoon chopped thyme

4 tablespoons chopped parsley

200g / 7oz feta cheese, crumbled

freshly ground black pepper

2–4 tablespoons fresh breadcrumbs

This is filling and nutritious – good for a chilly winter's day. Buttery cooked kale or cabbage goes well with it, or baked potatoes, which can be done in the oven at the same time (start them off first).

1 If you are using dried lentils, put them into a saucepan with plenty of cold water to cover them well, bring to the boil, then leave them to simmer gently for 40–45 minutes, until tender.

2 Fill a saucepan with 2 litres / 3½ pints of water and put it on the stove to heat up for the pasta.

3 When the water in the saucepan boils, add the pasta along with a tablespoon of salt and give the pasta a quick stir. Briefly put the lid on until it starts to lift, showing that the water has come back to the boil, then let the pasta bubble away, uncovered, for about 8 minutes, or until it is tender but still has some bite to it. Drain the pasta into a colander.

4 Set the oven to 200°C/400°F/gas 6. Grease a casserole dish or roasting tin about 20 x 30cm / 8 x 12 inches and at least 6cm / 2½ inches deep.

5 Meanwhile, heat the oil in a medium-sized saucepan and add the onion; cover and cook for 5 minutes. Add the garlic, carrots and celery; cover and cook gently for 5 minutes. Then add the leeks, cover and cook for a further 10 minutes, until all the vegetables are tender.

6 Drain the lentils and add to the pasta, along with the vegetable mixture, sun-dried tomatoes, thyme and parsley. Crumble in half the feta. Mix well and season with salt and pepper.

7 Spoon the mixture into the prepared casserole dish, scatter the remaining feta cheese and breadcrumbs on top, then bake for about 30 minutes, until golden brown.

MACARONI, CHEESE AND TOMATO BAKE Serves ❹

INGREDIENTS

225g / 8oz macaroni

salt

1 teaspoon made mustard

1 egg, separated

175g / 6oz Cheddar cheese, grated

1 quantity of béchamel sauce
(page 90)

freshly ground black pepper

450g / 1lb fresh tomatoes, sliced

A new version of an old favourite, this is good with a lightly cooked green vegetable or a salad.

1 Fill a large saucepan with 4 litres / 7 pints of water and put it on the stove to heat up for the pasta.

2 Set the oven to 200°C/400°F/gas 6. Grease a casserole dish or roasting tin about 20 x 30cm / 8 x 12 inches and at least 6cm / 2½ inches deep.

3 When the water boils, add the pasta along with a tablespoon of salt and give the pasta a quick stir. Briefly put the lid on until it starts to lift, showing that the water has come back to the boil, then let the pasta bubble away, uncovered, for about 8 minutes, or until it is tender but still has some bite to it. Drain the pasta.

4 Stir the mustard, egg yolk and 50g / 2oz of the cheese into the béchamel sauce in a mixing bowl. Add the drained pasta.

5 Whisk the egg white until it is stiff but not dry, then fold into the macaroni mixture, along with salt and pepper to taste.

6 Pour the mixture into the prepared dish and arrange the tomato slices over the top, placing them very close together. Scatter the cheese over the tomato slices, and bake for about 30 minutes, until the top is golden brown and the inside lightly set.

RIGATONI, LEEK AND RICOTTA CHEESE BAKE Serves ❹

INGREDIENTS

450g / 1lb leeks, trimmed and cut into 6mm / ¼ inch slices

225g / 8oz rigatoni

salt

225g / 8oz ricotta cheese

2 garlic cloves, peeled and crushed

8 tablespoons sun-dried tomato purée

4 tablespoons chopped parsley

50g / 2oz pitted black olives, sliced

freshly ground black pepper

50g / 2oz freshly grated Parmesan cheese

Another handy dish that can be quickly put together ahead of time and baked later when you need it. A juicy tomato salad with some fresh basil, or tomatoes roasted in the oven alongside the bake, complement it perfectly.

1 Fill a large saucepan with 4 litres / 7 pints of water and put it on the stove to heat up for the pasta.

2 Set the oven to 200°C/400°F/gas 6. Grease a casserole dish or roasting tin about 20 x 30cm / 8 x 12 inches and at least 6cm / 2½ inches deep.

3 Meanwhile, cook the leeks in a little boiling water for about 6 minutes until they are tender, then drain them.

4 When the water in the saucepan boils, add the pasta along with a tablespoon of salt and give the pasta a quick stir. Briefly put the lid on until it starts to lift, showing that the water has come back to the boil, then let the pasta bubble away, uncovered, for about 8 minutes, or until it is tender but still has some bite to it.

5 Drain the pasta, return to its pan and mix with the leeks, ricotta, garlic, sun-dried tomato purée, parsley, olives and salt and pepper to taste.

6 Spoon the mixture into the prepared dish, scatter the Parmesan cheese on top and bake for about 30 minutes, or until golden brown.

PEPPERS STUFFED WITH PASTA, TOMATO, OLIVES AND CHEESE Serves ❹ as a main course, ❽ as a starter

INGREDIENTS

125g / 4oz short macaroni
(or anelli or ruote di carro)

salt

1 tablespoon olive oil

1 small onion, peeled and chopped

125g / 4oz mushrooms, washed
and sliced

1 garlic clove, peeled and crushed

150ml / 5fl oz béchamel sauce
(¼ of recipe on page 90)

2 tomatoes, skinned, de-seeded
and chopped

50g / 2oz pitted black olives, sliced

125g / 4oz Cheddar or Gruyère
cheese, cut into 6mm / ¼ inch dice

freshly ground black pepper

4 medium-sized red peppers, halved
through the stems and de-seeded

You could use golden or green peppers equally as well as red ones for this dish, or, if you're making enough for a crowd, use a mixture of all three for a particularly colourful effect.

1 Fill a saucepan with 2 litres / 3½ pints of water and put it on the stove to heat up for the pasta.

2 Set the oven to 200°C/400°F/gas 6. Grease a casserole dish or roasting tin large enough to hold the peppers in a single layer.

3 When the water in the saucepan boils, add the pasta along with a tablespoon of salt and give the pasta a quick stir. Briefly put the lid on until it starts to lift, showing that the water has come back to the boil, then let the pasta bubble away, uncovered, for about 8 minutes, or until it is tender but still has some bite to it.

4 Meanwhile, heat the oil in a medium-sized saucepan and put in the onion; cover and cook for 5 minutes. Then add the mushrooms and garlic and cook, uncovered, for a further 5 minutes, until the onions and mushrooms are tender.

5 Drain the pasta and add to the mushroom and onion mixture, along with the béchamel sauce, tomatoes, olives, cheese and salt and pepper to taste.

6 Put the peppers, cut-side up, in the baking dish or tin and fill them with the pasta mixture, piling it up well. Bake them for about 40 minutes, until the peppers are tender when pierced with the point of a knife and the filling is golden brown. Serve two stuffed pepper halves per person as a main course, with a crisp green salad, or put each pepper half on a base of green leaves and serve to eight as a first course.

RICOTTA, SWEETCORN, BASIL AND PARMESAN CANNELLONI IN TOMATO SAUCE Serves ❹

INGREDIENTS

8 sheets of lasagne verde

salt

225g / 8oz ricotta cheese

225g / 8oz can sweetcorn, drained, or 175g / 6oz fresh or frozen sweetcorn kernels

2 tablespoons torn or chopped fresh basil leaves

125g / 4oz freshly grated Parmesan cheese

freshly ground black pepper

2 x quantity of tomato sauce (page 106)

Rather than use cannelloni tubes, which can be difficult to fill, I use sheets of lasagne, cut in half, and wrapped around a filling, such as this one.

1 Cook the lasagne in plenty of boiling, salted water for 6–8 minutes, or until tender but still with some bite. Drain and drape the lasagne sheets over the sides of the saucepan and a colander to prevent them from sticking together.

2 Set the oven to 200°C/400°F/gas 6. Grease a casserole dish or roasting tin about 20 x 30cm / 8 x 12 inches and at least 6cm / 2 ½ inches deep.

3 Next, make the filling. Mix together the ricotta cheese, sweetcorn (no need to cook it first), basil and half the Parmesan. Season with salt and pepper.

4 Lay one of the sheets of lasagne out on a board; spoon a line of the filling down the long side of the sheet, then roll it up to enclose the filling and make a cannelloni roll. Cut the roll in half and place in the casserole dish. Repeat using the remaining sheets of lasagne and filling, making two layers.

5 Pour the tomato sauce over the pasta, scatter with the remaining Parmesan and bake for 35–40 minutes, until golden brown.

MUSHROOMS STUFFED WITH ORECCHIETTE, OLIVES AND CAPERS Serves ❹ as a main course, ❽ as a starter

INGREDIENTS

olive oil

1 onion, peeled and chopped

1 garlic clove, peeled and crushed

125g / 4oz orecchiette

salt

150ml / 5fl oz béchamel sauce (¼ of recipe on page 90)

4 sun-dried tomatoes, chopped

50g / 2oz pitted black olives, sliced

2 tablespoons capers

1 tablespoon chopped fresh parsley

freshly ground black pepper

8 large flat mushrooms

50g / 2oz freshly grated Parmesan

Any small pasta shapes can be used for this recipe, which makes a piquant snack or first course.

1 Heat 1 tablespoon of olive oil in a saucepan and put in the onion; cover and cook for 5 minutes. Add the garlic and cook, uncovered, for a further 5 minutes.

2 Fill a saucepan with 2 litres / 3½ pints of water and put it on the stove to heat up. When the water boils, add the pasta along with a tablespoon of salt and give the pasta a quick stir. Briefly put the lid on until it starts to lift, showing that the water has come back to the boil, then let the pasta bubble away, uncovered, for about 8 minutes, or until it is tender but still has some bite to it.

3 Drain the pasta and add to the onion mixture, along with the béchamel sauce, sun-dried tomatoes, olives, capers, parsley and salt and pepper to taste. Keep it warm.

4 Wipe the mushrooms and trim the stalks so that they are level with the black gills. Brush lightly with olive oil, season and place, black side up, on a grill pan. Partially cook under a hot grill for 3–5 minutes. Remove from the heat.

5 Pile the stuffing mixture on top of the mushrooms, dividing it evenly, and scatter with the Parmesan. Place under the hot grill for 5–10 minutes, until golden brown.

SPINACH AND RICOTTA CANNELLONI IN TOMATO SAUCE Serves ❹

This is excellent as either a starter or a main course. A salad of grated carrot, fennel and black olives goes well with it.

1 Cook the lasagne in plenty of boiling, salted water for 6–8 minutes, or until tender but still with some bite. Drain and drape the lasagne sheets over the sides of the saucepan and a colander to prevent them from sticking together.

2 Set the oven to 200°C/400°F/gas 6. Grease a casserole dish or roasting tin about 20 x 30cm / 8 x 12 inches and at least 6cm / 2½ inches deep.

3 Next, make the filling. Melt the butter in a large saucepan and put in the spinach. Cook for 5–6 minutes, or until the spinach is tender, pushing it down into the pan and chopping it with the end of a fish slice or spatula. Drain off any excess water, then add the ricotta cheese, half the Parmesan and a good seasoning of salt, pepper and nutmeg.

4 Lay one of the sheets of lasagne out on a board; spoon a line of the filling down the long side of the sheet, then roll it up to enclose the filling and make a cannelloni roll. Cut the roll in half and place in the casserole dish. Repeat using the remaining sheets of lasagne and filling, making two layers of cannelloni in the dish.

5 Pour the tomato sauce over the cannelloni, scatter with the remaining Parmesan and bake for 35–40 minutes, until golden brown.

MUSHROOM CANNELLONI IN BÉCHAMEL SAUCE Serves ❹

INGREDIENTS

8 sheets of lasagne

salt

1 tablespoon olive oil

25g / 1oz butter

700g / 1½lb mushrooms, washed and chopped

150g / 5oz full-fat or low-fat garlic and herb cream cheese

2 tablespoons chopped fresh parsley

freshly ground black pepper

75g / 3oz freshly grated Parmesan cheese

1 quantity of béchamel sauce (page 90)

You could use tomato sauce instead of béchamel for this dish if you prefer.

1 Cook the lasagne in plenty of boiling, salted water for 6–8 minutes, or until tender but still with some bite. Drain and drape the lasagne sheets over the sides of the saucepan and a colander to prevent them from sticking together.

2 Set the oven to 200°C/400°F/gas 6. Grease a casserole dish or roasting tin about 20 x 30cm / 8 x 12 inches and at least 6cm / 2½ inches deep.

3 Next, make the filling. Heat the olive oil and butter in a saucepan, then add the mushrooms and cook over quite a high heat for about 10 minutes or until tender and any liquid has boiled away. Remove from the heat and add the cream cheese, chopped parsley and salt and pepper to taste.

4 Lay one of the sheets of lasagne out on a board; spoon a line of the filling down the long side of the sheet, then roll it up to enclose the filling and make a cannelloni roll. Cut the roll in half and place in the casserole dish. Repeat using the remaining sheets of lasagne and filling, making two layers of cannelloni in the dish.

5 Add half of the Parmesan to the béchamel sauce, then pour over the cannelloni. Scatter with the remaining Parmesan and bake for 35–40 minutes, until golden brown.

LEEK AND GOAT'S CHEESE CANNELLONI IN TOMATO SAUCE Serves ❹

INGREDIENTS

8 sheets of lasagne

salt

700g / 1½lb leeks, trimmed and cut into 6mm / ¼ inch slices

125g / 4oz soft goat's cheese

freshly ground black pepper

2 x quantity of tomato sauce (page 106)

25g / 1oz freshly grated Parmesan cheese

This is a very good combination of flavours and colours – delicious with steamed broccoli and crusty bread.

1 Cook the lasagne in plenty of boiling, salted water for 6–8 minutes, or until tender but still with some bite. Drain and drape the lasagne sheets over the sides of the saucepan and a colander to prevent them from sticking together.

2 Set the oven to 200°C/400°F/gas 6. Grease a casserole dish or roasting tin about 20 x 30cm / 8 x 12 inches and at least 6cm / 2½ inches deep.

3 Next, make the filling. Cook the leeks in a little boiling water until they are just tender: about 6 minutes. Drain, and combine with the goat's cheese. Season with salt and pepper to taste.

4 Lay one of the sheets of lasagne out on a board; spoon a line of the filling down the long side of the sheet, then roll it up to enclose the filling and make a cannelloni roll. Cut the roll in half and place in the casserole dish. Repeat using the remaining sheets of lasagne and filling, making two layers of cannelloni in the dish.

5 Pour the tomato sauce over the cannelloni, scatter with the Parmesan and bake for 35–40 minutes, until golden brown.

STUFFED AUBERGINE SLICES WITH BÉCHAMEL Serves ❹

INGREDIENTS

2 medium-sized aubergines

salt

125g / 4oz short pasta
(not macaroni)

olive oil

150ml / 5fl oz tomato sauce (½ of
recipe on page 106)

1 tablespoon sun-dried tomato purée

2–3 good sprigs of basil, torn

freshly ground black pepper

300ml / 10fl oz béchamel sauce
(½ of recipe on page 90)

50g / 2oz freshly grated
Parmesan cheese

Thick luscious slices of aubergine, sandwiched with a tasty mixture of pasta, basil and sun-dried tomatoes and baked in a béchamel sauce with a topping of Parmesan cheese, make an excellent, substantial main course.

1 First cut a thin slice from each side of the aubergine: these will not be needed. Then cut each aubergine downwards so that you have four thick slices from each one. Put the slices into a colander, sprinkle with salt and leave for an hour to draw out any bitter juices and also to prevent the aubergine from absorbing too much oil when you fry it. Then rinse the aubergine under the tap and squeeze it dry.

2 Fill a saucepan with 2 litres / 3½ pints of water and put it on the stove to heat up for the pasta.

3 Set the oven to 200°C/400°F/gas 6. Grease a casserole dish or roasting tin large enough to take the four aubergine slices in a single layer.

4 When the water in the saucepan boils, add the pasta along with a tablespoon of salt and give the pasta a quick stir. Briefly put the lid on until it starts to lift, showing that the water has come back to the boil, then let the pasta bubble away, uncovered, for about 8 minutes, or until it is tender but still has some bite to it.

5 Meanwhile, fry the aubergine slices in a little olive oil, on both sides, until tender and lightly browned. Or brush them on both sides with olive oil and grill until tender.

6 Drain the pasta, return to the still-warm pan and add the tomato sauce, sun-dried tomato purée, basil and salt and pepper.

7 Put four slices of aubergine in the baking dish or tin. Top each with the pasta mixture, dividing it evenly between them, then top each with another slice of aubergine. Spoon the béchamel sauce over the top of the aubergine 'sandwiches', scatter with Parmesan cheese and bake for about 30 minutes, until golden brown.

Index

······ · · · · · · · · · · · · ······